BOJIDAR DIMITROV

BULGARIANS – THE FIRST EUROPEANS

ST. KLIMENT OHRIDSKI UNIVERSITY PRESS

Our contribution in the publication of this book is a respect for the faith, honour, wisdom, heroism and talent of the Bulgarian who is deeply inlaid into the European system of values.

Reni and Petar Manjukov

BOJIDAR DIMITROV

BULGARIANS – THE FIRST EUROPEANS

St. Kliment Ohridski University Press
Sofia • 2002

ISBN 954-07-1758-2

PREFACE

The contemporary state of Bulgaria covers Europe's south-east corner. Its territory is 111 000 square kilometres and population about 9 million people. Bulgaria is on 12-13th place among the fifty European states concerning territory and population, but is quite unknown to the European world. It is hardly the right place here to look for the reasons for this fact. However, the main reason may lie in the circumstance that Bulgaria and the Bulgarians have not "produced" for the last fifty years "bad" news, which would put the country and its citizens on to the top of news agencies' and media's prime-time. In Bulgaria, during the period of communist rule (1944–1989) Czech, Hungarian or Polish events did not happen (which, according to some people is not so good). The transition to democracy and market economy has also been peaceful and calm without bloodshed that turned in red the transition in Romania and Russia. Bulgaria has avoided the civil war too, which is still shaking neighbouring Yugoslavia. In Bulgaria, there are no ethnical and religious problems, despite the fact that considerable percent of its citizens belong to different ethnical minorities and several religions are professed (Orthodoxy, Catholicism, Islam and Judaism). The specialists in this area even start talking about Bulgarian ethnical model, ensuring peace, understanding and co-operation between ethnical and religious communities. This is interesting for the specialists, but not for the editors-in-chief of newspapers and magazines.

But sadly At least in the countries from the European Union, whose member Bulgaria will be in several years, more about the history of Bulgarian lands, Bulgarians and Bulgaria should be known. And if not about all, at least the fact that the first highly developed civilisation appears in Vth millennium exactly in the present Bulgarian lands and whose creators are in some sense the first Europeans. It is also necessary to know the main contributions made by the Bulgarians and Bulgarian State during the Middle Ages – the epoch in which foundations of the contemporary European Civilisation are laid. This is also the concept of nation state, successfully implemented in VII–XIVth centuries, which has become model for Europe's development instead of the concept of universal Christian state, as well as the much more successful mission of the Bulgarians in the Slavic world World that even in these days covers approximately half of the European territory and population.

The author has written this book, precisely led by the thought that it is necessary for some gaps to be filled in the knowledge of the average European about Bulgaria and the Bulgarians.

Ruler's signs of power (insignias) from the Varna Chalcolithic Necropolis, Vth millennium BC, gold, copper, bone.

Thracians – The First Europeans

Chapter I

The contemporary Bulgarian people was formed in VI–IXth C. by the merger of three peoples–the Thracians, the Slavs and the Bulgarians. The Thracians were the local indigenous population among them. Both the Slavs and Bulgarians came to the present Bulgarian territories in V–VIIth C. AD, during the Great Migration of Peoples.

The Thracians were mentioned in the written sources of information from XIIIth C. BC as an independent people, in connection with their participation in the Trojan War as allies of the Trojans.

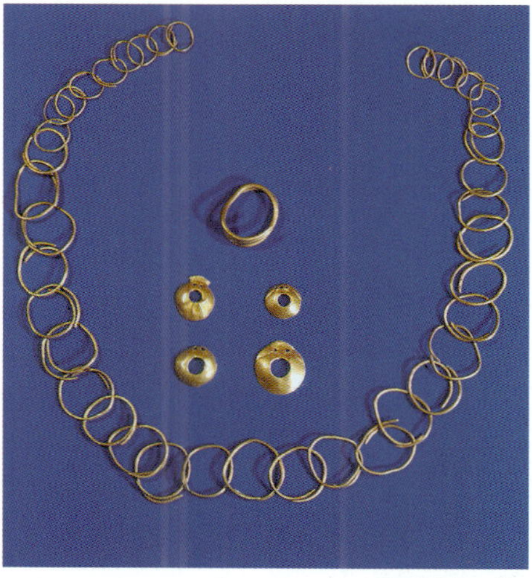

Golden treasure from Hotnitza, V–IVth millennium BC

Golden rhyton from Thracian treasure, discovered near Panagyurishte, IVth C. BC

Their origin and their appearance in the Balkans were question at issue for the science until recently. The scientists discussed whether they were products of the independent development of the indigenous people from the Neolithic, the Copper and the Bronze Ages, or they were newcomers from the South or the North.

Golden rhyton from Thracian treasure, discovered near Panagyurishte, IVth C. BC

An ancient necropolis dating back to V–VIth millennium was discovered thirty years ago, during some construction works near the town of Varna – big Bulgarian port on the Black Sea Coast. Some of the buried persons had amazing golden and copper grave offerings – solid golden bracelets, appliqués, golden sceptre-symbol of the ruler' power. At the same time, the finds from the European necropolis did not consist of anything, but primitive ceramics and utensils made of stone and clay. The presence of class society and strict hierarchy in strata was a mark of highly-developed civilisation. The world science thought until recently that the fireplaces of the first human civilisation blazed up for the first time in Asia Minor, in the valleys of both, the Tigris and Euphrates, Palestine and Egypt. Nowadays, it is clear that the civilisation fireplace of the human groups near Varna from the Vth millennium, existed parallel to those civilisation fireplaces, and perhaps short before them. And not only near Varna. The intensified excavation works of the Bulgarian archaeologists in the following years, showed that the first high developed civilisation in Europe comprised a vast area in some part of present East and South Bulgaria. The American scientist Dr. Robert Ballard thinks that large part of the golden civilisation in Varna was engulfed in the Black Sea waters. But so far, his expeditions have not confirmed his statement.

Golden rhyton from Thracian treasure, discovered near Panagyurishte, IVth C. BC

The excavation works of villages and necropolises dating from V–IIIth millennium BC, proved that the development of human groups from that age was uninterrupted by foreign invasions. It was they that had formed the Thracian people noticed by the great Homer in II Millennium. Based on that fact conclusion is made that exactly the Thracians are the creators of the first high-

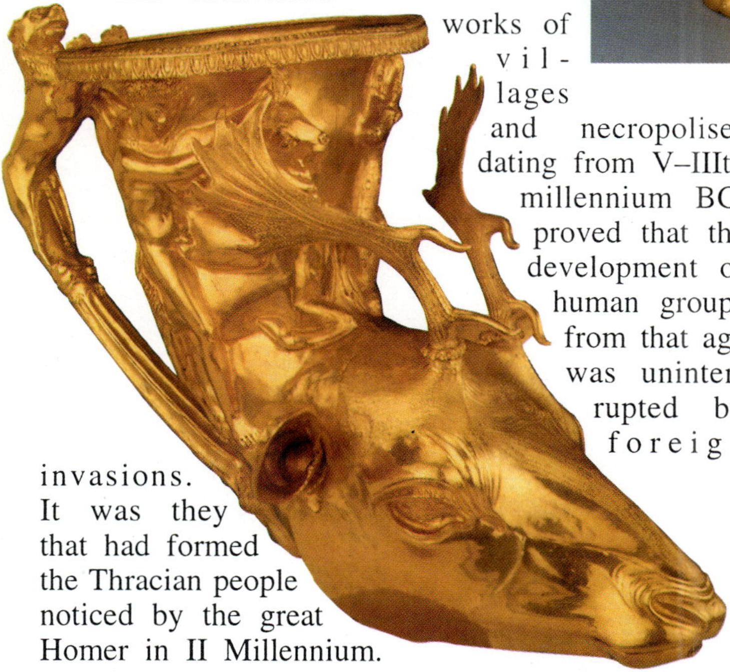

Golden rhyton from Thracian treasure, discovered in Panagyurishte, IVth C. BC

Thracian rock sanctuary at Perperikhon fortress, Kurjali region, IIth millennium BC

Thracian rock sanctuary at Perperikhon fortress, Kurjali region, IIth millennium BC

Thracian rock sanctuary at Perperikhon fortress, Kurjali region, IIth millennium BC

The church "St. George" situated in downtown of the Bulgarian capital, IV–VIth C. AD

Thracian temple-tomb near the village of Starossel, Plovdiv region, Vth C. BC

Golden rhyton from Thracian treasure, discovered near Panagyurishte, IVth C. BC

Golden amphora from Thracian treasure discovered near the town of Panagyurishte, IVth C. BC

ly developed civilisation in Europe. Therefore, there is a certain reason the Thracians to be named the first Europeans.

Golden phiale rom Thracian treasure discovered near the town of Panagyurishte, IVth C. BC

The Thracian ethnos' borders comprised not only the territory of present-day Bulgaria, but also the lands of present-day Romania, Eastern Serbia, Northern Greece and North-west Turkey. According to the Greek historian Herodotus (Vth C. BC) the Thracians were the most numerous people in

Europe and the second in the world after the Hindus (naturally the world that Herodotus knew).

Unfortunately, the Thracians did not create their own alphabet during their two thousand-year-history. The restoration of the past of this people – builder of one of the pillars of the ancient European civilisation was based on the scanty information left by both, the Hellenes and Romans in their literary traditions. Naturally, it was also based on the results obtained from the archaeological excavations that reached particularly large scale over the last three-four decades.

The production of foods, raw materials and other goods that had fully satisfied the local needs and that had produced considerable overstock addressed to all the directions, was

Golden rhyton from Thracian treasure discovered near the town of Panagyurishte, IVth C. BC

Silver jug from Thracian treasure discovered in Rogozen, IVth C. BC

Silver rhyton from theThracian treasure discovered in the village of Borovo, IVth C. BC

Thracian rhyton from the treasure discovered in the village of Borovo, IVth C. BC

certainly the basis of the Thracian economy during the early centuries of the Thracian people's development. It could be particularly easy to follow the path of the Thracian export southeastward and southward i.e. to the peoples inhabiting Asia Minor, the Near East and the Aegean Sea shore. The stock exchange was carried out mostly by sea through the Thracian harbours to Phoenicia, Egypt, Caria, Crete and Mycenae. It inevitably resulted in intensified exchange of people, political and cultural ideas as well as technological information. All that caused revolution in the social and political reality of Thrace and the Thracians.

Apparently the social differentiation in Thrace gained speed too early (as early as the second half of II millennium BC). It caused the emerging of the early-class social formations. This process concerned all the

Golden cup from Vratza, IVth C. BC

Thracian tribes, whose number was several dozens. Their social structure was simple. The chief-ruler, who was also supreme priest, was on the top of the social pyramid. He exercised his power over the level of free community farmers and artisans through the suite of close aristocrats. Bondage did not find wide application in the Thracian economy besides, to some extent, in the few royal domains. This structure of the Thracian society had practically not been modified in the course of more than 15 centuries until the Romans conquered Thrace in Ist C. AD.

By the beginning of XIII Th C. BC, some of the Thracian state formations comprising the territorial and ethnic borders of the particular tribes had already been noticed by the ancient authors in connection with the Trojan War. They were linked to the lands of South Thrace and became Trojan allies, with whom they had already had economic, political and probably ethnical relations. King Rhezus was one of the rulers

Amphora (silver with gilt), IVth C. BC

Small jug from the Thracian treasure, discovered in Rogozen, IVth C. BC

Silver jug from the Thracian treasure, discovered in Rogozen, IVth C. BC

Silver phiale from the Thracian treasure, discovered in Rogozen, IVth C. BC

Silver phiale from the Thracian treasure, discovered in Rogozen, IVth C. BC

from this zone famous for his influence and wealth. He was also famous for his tragic fate – killed by Ulysses in his camp, before taking part in the combats near Troy.

Silver phiale from the Thracian treasure, discovered in Rogozen, IVth C. BC

The political independence of the Thracian tribes was kept until the beginning of Vth C. BC. Then Teres, the ruler of one of their tribes, made a successful attempt to organise one unified Thracian state. All the Thracian tribes inhabiting the present Bulgarian territories were unified within the Odrissian Kingdom's boundaries during the rule of Sparadokus, Sitalkus and Sevtum (Vth C. BC). As Athens allies in the Peloponnesian war, the Odryssian rulers awed the enemies of the antique democracy in its northern zone of influence, by providing Athens regular grain supply, supply of raw materials and metals. During the same Vth C. BC, the Odryssian rulers crushed the Macedonian attempts to appear on the great political scene. However, in the middle of the following century (IVth C. BC), the Macedonians got their revenge through Philip and Alexander the Great. The Odryssian Kingdom endured some harsh blows and its boundaries shrunk into comparatively small region in the Upper Thracian Lowland. In the rapidly changing political situation between the end of IVth and the beginning of Ist C. BC, some new Thracian states emerged on the political arena in Thrace. The states of the Bessae, Astae, Getae, Daceans enjoyed a brilliant but

Golden vessel from the Thracian treasure, discovered near the village of Vulchitran, VIIIth C. BC

transient political success. The struggles for political leadership between the Thracian family dynasties facilitated the offensive of Rome, which succeeded in imposing its domination over the Thracian people in 46 AD, after series of sanguinary wars and complicated diplomatic combinations. In the vicissitudes of this almost two-century-long resistance, Spartacus was captured and turned into gladiator. He was the Thracian to raise the biggest slaves' uprising of the Antique World, which nearly caused the downfall of Rome.

The ancient theatre in Plovdiv,
I–IIIth C. AD

Within the boundaries of the Roman Empire, most of the Thracian lands were organised into two big provinces-Moesia and Thracia. They both lived out the Thracians. Nowadays, two of the three vast Bulgarian historical areas (Moesia, Thracia and Macedonia) bear their names. After the sanguinary decades of conquest, years of peaceful labour and calm set in the Thracian lands. The Thracians soon obtained full civil rights of Roman citizens. Agriculture and cattle breeding kept on being the basis of the main occupation. The production remained in the hands of the free community peasants. The immense Italian latifundii, where tens of thousands slaves worked, were unknown phenomenon in Thrace.

Bronze figurine
of a Thracian horseman,
II–IIIth C. AD

During the first two centuries (I–IIIth C. AD), the Roman authorities built well constructed roads in the lands of ancient Thrace. Nowadays, some of their beds coincide with the European road network system. Dozens of well-built towns with developed crafts and industry (on the social base of free artisans) emerged. They had cultural institutions and high developed urban infrastructure. The Thracians entered the state administration. Some of them reached high administrative and military appointments. Sometimes, the Thracians held even the emperor's throne. The name of Maximinus (235–238) led the series of Thracian-Roman emperors. He was a Thracian peasant, who in a short period of time progressed from the short sword a of trainee in the Roman legions to the divine August's sceptre.

The nearly idyllic picture of life in the Bulgarian lands was destroyed in the middle of IIIth C. AD. The following waves of barbaric invasions that traced the Great Migration's march hit this flourishing region of the Roman Empire in a terrifying methodical manner. Tens of peoples coming from the present frozen Russian steppes and swamps, or from the Asian deserts, broke through the system of Roman frontier fortifications. (According to the fragments of remaining written and epigraphic sources, the Bulgarian historians counted 54 peoples attacking on these lands between III–Vth C. AD).

After smashing the resistance of both the legions and garrisons of the towns, the Barbarians robbed the provinces' wealth, started killing and kidnapping people, and destroyed the provinces and the brilliant Roman-Thracian civilisation. The Roman authori-

Thracian chariot – fragment of the mural in the tumulus near Kazanluk, IVth C. BC

Mural painting from Thracian tomb situated near Aleksandrovo village, Vth C. BC

Mural painting from Thracian tomb situated near Aleksandrovo village, Vth C. BC

Mural paintings from Thracian tomb situated near Aleksandrovo village, Ith C. BC

Thracian system of rock sanctuaries near Stranjevo village, Kurjali region,
XIII–XIIth C. BC

Thracian temple-tomb situated near Starossel village, VIth C. BC

Mural decoration of Thracian king's tumulus near the town of Kazanluk, IVth C. BC

ties made great efforts to stop the destructive barbaric impact. Many fortresses and roads were restored. New others were built. In the ravaged regions, barbaric tribes were made settle as "federates". These efforts doubled, after the Empire was divided into two parts and the capital established in Constantinople. The Bulgarian lands were an immediate hinterland of the one-million city.

Thracian queen-fragment of mural painting in a tumulus near the town of Kazanluk IVth C. BC

But all the efforts were in vain. The barbaric blows followed one after another. The ancient civilisation of Moesia and Thrace was destroyed at the beginning of VIIth C. The life in the existing towns and villages became rustic and barbarian. After the Thracians suffered considerable demographic losses, they had practically disappeared from the historical scene. Small groups survived somewhere in the high inaccessible mountains, others withdrew to the big well-fortified Imperial city centres situated out of the present Bulgarian lands. There, the Roman power was absolutely titular; it was not represented anywhere but just in few city centres that had emerged as isolated islands on the stormy barbaric sea.

It seemed that these lands would never become field of peaceful cre-

Procession – fragment of mural painting in a tumulus near the town of Kazanluk, IVth C. BC

ative life. But on the roads in the Northern Regions of the Balkan Peninsula, the steps of one people, to whom history granted the right to bring Thrace, Mosea and Macedonia back to the bosom of the the European Civilisation, had already echoed hollowly back. The Bulgarians inhabiting the valleys between the Caucasus, the Black Sea and Caspian Sea kept intact and even increased their human, economic and military potential, in spite of the reverses of fortune. It was exactly they to have the historic chance to found the Bulgarian State.

The church "St. Erasmo" near Ohrid, VI C.

Golden buckle from belt of the founder of Bulgaria, Khan Kubrat, 632

Decoration of the sword of the founder of Bulgaria, Khan Kubrat, 632.

The Slavs

Chapter II

The homeland of this tribe that nowadays inhabits a huge part of the earth – from Vladivostok to the Odder and from the Arctic Ocean to the Adriatic, was in Central Europe. Both, the ancient Greek and Roman authors situated them in the valleys, forests and swamps between the Odder, the Wisla and the Baltic Sea. In the south, the Slavs touched the inter-river areas of the Bug and the Dnestre, as well as the Carpathian crest.

According to the Roman historian Tacitus, the Slavic way of living and their racial type were similar to the German ones. They were blond and well-built people leading a settled life and earning their bread on primitive agriculture, cattle-breeding, hunting and....even robbery. Their social system was characterised by the domination of the family communities; they used to unify temporarily (and not necessarily all of them), for a joint temporary operation – for example an armed incursion on the frontier areas of the Roman Empire. At this age, the Slavs did not have any state formations.

Their migration toward all the European directions started at the end of IVth C. AD. We could just try to guess the reasons for this huge demographic explosion that resulted in immense human waves scattering over the present German, Ukrainian, Russian, Belorussian, Hungarian, Romanian, Czech, Croatian, Serbian, Greek and Bulgarian lands.

In a short period of time, the Slavs took over and settled in Europe as far as the Elba River in the west, the Ural and the Volga in the east and the Danube in the south. Even nowadays, the historians wonder at this irresistible rush. Perhaps, they left many casualties in their invasions. They had no cavalry, no protective means and their attacking weaponry was quite primitive.

The Slavic ground squads started appearing south of the Danube in the decades about the end of IVth – the beginning of Vth C. It seemed that they were the loosing party there. South of the Danube, the flourishing regions of the East Roman Empire (Bizantium) were situated. Byzantium was populous. There were thousands of perfectly built fortresses connected with each other by roads, as well as garrisons armed to the teeth. Nevertheless, something incredible had happened – the Slavs managed to break trough all the defensive lines and conquer the whole Balkan

Golden buckle from belt of Khan Kubrat, the founder of Bulgaria, 632

Fortress wall of the aristocratic quarter in the Bulgarian capital Pliska, 681–893

Golden ring-seal of the founder of Bulgaria, Khan Kubrat, 632

Peninsula just in hundreds of years despite their own terrible losses. From Trieste to Varna and from the Danube to Peloponnesus. Right, even to Peloponnesus. The Slavic tribes settled in even there, as well as all over Hellas. The brilliant civilisation of the Roman Empire irrevocably collapsed forever. Huge roman towns turned into deserts. Churches, amphitheatres, roads and villas became overgrown with thorns and bushes. Countless of straw huts and dugout dwellings had emerged on their former places. They belonged to the blond newcomers who had rapidly assimilated the thinning Thracian population. At the end of Vth C. AD, Constantinople and Thessalonica, still governed by the Eastern Roman Empire, stayed erected as lonely islands on the Slavic

Entrance in the fortress wall of the Bulgarian capital Pliska, 681–893

sea, sieged and terrorised in every 10–15 years by the notorious Slavic raids, which had been picturesquely described by the church writers in the numerous martyr's biographies.

But the Slavs could not found their own state neither on the Balkans nor anywhere in both, the homeland and new-conquered territories. The strong tribal

Altar part in the so-called "Big basilica" in the Bulgarian capital Pliska, built in 865 by Tsar Boris I. The big basilica, 99 m. long and 30 m. large, was the biggest Christian temple in Medieval Europe

aspiration for independence drowned each state-forming idea in its foetal stage. All over the Slavic world, the states were founded centuries later by foreign tribes, which had been too different by language, way of living and race from the Slavs. In Czechia – by a Franc merchant, whose name was Samo, in Poland – by the Germans, in Russia – by the Normans with Swedish origin.

In the lands, situated south of the Danube, it would be done by the Bulgarians.

Golden jug with image of a Bulgarian warrior, from medieval Bulgarian treasure, VIIIth C. AD

Fragment from "The big basilica" in Pliska, 865

The Bulgarians

Chapter III

The foundation of the Bulgarian State on the territories crowded with numerous tribes of many languages is connected with the Bulgarians. For the sake of convenience, the present historians call them "ante-Bulgarians" or "proto-Bulgarians" in order to distinguish them from the Bulgarian people formed in IX–Xth C. on Slavic linguistic base. They call themselves Bulgarians. This is the name which all the Byzantines and all the people at that age call them. Therefore, we will just call them Bulgarians. The Francs, who have founded Ancient France, are Germans, but the large part of its population is consisted of Gauloromans, this is the language that they still speak today but the French historians have never called them "proto-French". The same is in Russia. The Norman tribe Russians that has never had anything in common with the Slavs, has not been named by the Russian geographers "ante or proto-Russians".

* * *

Both, the origin and homeland of the Bulgarian tribes have always been object of studying in the past and the present days, have raised and raise many hypothesis and violent disputes. And probably it will be like this for a long time. The scarcity of clear and reliable sources may hardly be filled.

Nevertheless, many Bulgarian scientists studying Armenian and Hindu sources accepted in the last years of XXth. C. unanimously the statement that the Bulgarians had inhabited the valleys and lowlands north of the Pamirs at least since VIIth. BC. This area was named by the ancient sources "the mountain Imeon". It included the fertile fields of Northern Afghanistan. In the past this region was called Balchari i.e. Bulgaria. Many sounds typical of the Bulgarian language even now determine in the same way the pronunciation of the Bulgarian State's name. The major Bulgarian city was Balch. Nowadays, a town which bears the same name, still exists in Northern Afghanistan.

According to the same sources the Bulgarians were Aryans of the Iranian racial and linguistic group. In the last quarter of IVth C. BC, the phalanxes of Alexander the Great rushed into Balchara region, which had been a part of Bactria-vassal of the enormous Persian Empire. The Bulgarians offered stern resistance and Alexander was forced to look for an agreement. Balchara accepted to be included in Alexander's Empire but if being allowed to keep some self-governing. Ten thousand Macedonians got married to local girls in order to strengthen the agreement. The Empire of Alexander of Macedonia

The horseman from Madara. Rock relief, carved by the Bulgarian Khan Tervel (701–716) in honour of the military victory over Byzantium in 705

"Tsar Boris I is accepting the Holy Christening"-miniature in Bulgarian manuscript from 1345

"S.S. Cyril and Methodius" – icon, XIXth C. AD

disintegrated as soon as he died in 323 and the Macedonian warriors stayed forever in Balchara's lands. Their Bulgarian descendants kept in their minds the memories of the antique Macedonian ancestors until the Late Middle Ages. Perhaps the Bulgarians were motivated by these fact when declared themselves as heirs of the Ancient Macedonians, as many Bulgarian and Greek works reported.

It seemed that the Bulgarian tribes were numerous enough. Between II and VIth. C.AD, considerable masses of at least three noticeable waves marched towards Europe. They suffered serious losses in the so-called Barbaric attacks on the Roman domains in the Old Continent and in internecine clashes. Nevertheless, their demographic resources had allowed them to found two mighty states-the first situated along the Volga, the second – along the Danube and to settle in whole areas of other state formations.

Ceramic icon of St. Theodor Stratilat, discovered in Preslav, Xth C. AD

Since IIth. C., some Bulgarian tribes had already stepped on the European continent and settled in the valleys between the Caspian and the Black Seas. One European chronicler noticed them right there for the first time in 354. According to the so-called Anonymous Roman Chronograph, their south border was fixed on the Caucasus crest. The snowy Caucasus dents did not stop them. The Armenian historian Moses of Horen had noticed that between 351 and 389, the Bulgarian tribes led by their leader Vund passed trough Caucasus and went to Armenia. According to some toponimic data they stayed there forever and the Armenians assimilated them hundreds of years later.

Other numerous Barbaric tribes left their homes in Northern Afghanistan carried away by the Huns' wave, which was going towards Europe at the beginning of IVth C. They settled in the lands along the Don and Donets Rivers and the Azovian Sea, where they assimilated on their turn the remains of the ancient Sarmatian tribes. Some of the tribes stayed for a long time in their new living places. The others together with the Huns continued their march to

Central Europe. They settled in both Panonia and Carphatian valleys. The union of Bulgarians and Huns lasted during the whole period of Hun's hegemony over Central Europe i.e. between 377–453. It was true that their name was rarely mentioned by the European authors of that time. The invaders spreading over Europe like a dark cloud were identified with the collective notion "Huns". However, the serious contemporary researchers may have right in their statement that the crucial striking power of Atila's troops come mainly from the Bulgarian cavalry.

The ancient Bulgarians did not put fortuitously Avitokhol and Irnik at the top of the genealogy of khan Kubrat's dynasty of statesmen.

Golden reliquary cross, discovered in the Bulgarian capital (between 681–893) Pliska

The Miniature "Tsar Boris is sending envoys to the Byzantine empress Theodora", Greek manuscript, XII C. AD

Obviously they were both identified respectively with the famous Hun chief Atila and his son Ernakh.

Indeed some West-European authors mentioned the Bulgarians during that epoch. Usually it happened mostly when battles were described. Nowadays, we could just try to guess why both the Panonian and Carpathian Bulgarians did not get on with the Langobards but the frequent wars between them were a fact. Actually we knew thanks to them that the Bulgarians cruelly defeated the Langobards in battle, then killed their king Agelmundi and captured his daughter. Then, they inflicted a stunning blow to the new Langobardian king Lamission.

The defeat of the Huns in the Catalonian fields caused the dissolution of the Hun-Bulgarian alliance and the Bulgarians independent manifestation on the international arena. In 480, Byzantium, which was looking forward to using the Bulgarians as allies in the difficult war with the attacking East Goths, concluded its first treaty with them. An enthusiastic eulogy of the East Goths' leader written by the East-Goths poet Enodius, revealed what kind of image the Bulgarian army enjoyed at that age. It was a story about the East Goth leader who had just slightly injured the Bulgarian commander-in-chief in a battle. The Bulgarians were described in this eulogy as supermen and invincible warriors.

In 488 the Goths, pushed by both the Byzantines and Bulgarians, drew off the Balkans forever. However, the bad days for Byzantium were still forthcoming. The Bulgarians had the opportunity to walk freely over Moesia, Thracia and Macedonia

St. Cyril, creator of the Bulgarian alphabet, mural painting in Vatican Apostolic Library, XIX C. AD

Miniatures with episodes from the wars of Bulgaria with Byzantium at the beginning of IX C. AD in Bulgarian manuscript dating from 1345

during their eight-year-long campaign as Byzantine allies against the Goths. Obviously they had liked these lands.

So the era of Bulgarian raids on the European imperial domains begun.

Just five years after throwing out the Goths, the Bulgarian army rushed into Thracia, defeated the Byzantine troops and killed their commander Julianus. The new horrifying danger was felt in Byzantium and the Emperor Anastasius I manifested unprecedented activity in the construction of fortresses. However, the new Bulgarian attack in 499 caused him a new humiliating rout. The whole Illirian army died in the battle of Tsurta River. In 502 AD the Bulgarians took over the whole Thracia again and ravaged it.

Since 513 AD, the Bulgarian attacks on the European Imperial domains came every year. Since 540 AD a basically new feature appeared. The Bulgarians were no longer satisfied with just robbing and kidnapping the rustic localities' populations, but started to take fortresses by using the siege techniques. In this way, they succeeded in seizing 32 of the fortresses just in Illiricum and kidnapping their population together with abundant spoil together. It was more than clear, that as the matters went Illiricum, Thracia, Moesia and Macedonia would turn into ravaged lands with no population and even the Bulgarians would settle in instead at the end of VI C. AD. Byzantium was fortunate because its diplomacy succeeded in provoking internecine wars between the two most powerful Bulgarian tribal branches-the Kutrigurs and Otigurs. It temporarily stopped the

Miniature in Greek manuscript – St. St. Cyril and Methodius are handing over the relics of pope Clement in Rome, XIV C. AD

Bulgarian raids on Byzantium. The last one, as noticed by the chronicler, was dated from 562 AD. The Slavic tribes had chance to settle in the present Bulgarian lands during the following five or six decades.

The participation of the Bulgarian tribes in joint operations with other peoples would disperse many of the Bulgarians who had settled in Central Europe. Therefore, when the Langobardic king Alboin took over three vast regions (568–569) in Northern Italy-Liguria, Lombard and Etruria-the population that he transferred there was not consisted of Langobardic tribes solely, but also of allied

Column with inscription, Pliska, VIIIth C. AD

The Golden church in the ancient Bulgarian capital Preslav, built by tsar Simeon the Great (893– 927)

Column with military victory inscription, Pliska, IXth C. AD

Bulgarian Tribes from Panonia. Many Italian families such, as "Bulgari" and "Bulgarini" (even nowadays they are widespread in Italy) became a souvenir from the Bulgarians brought by Alboin, who were later assimilated by the Italian people.

Other Bulgarian tribes, included in the Avarian khanate, took part in the Avarian campaigns against Byzantium. In 631–632 AD, they launched fierce struggle aiming to take over the supreme power in the khanate. They were defeated and as a result 9000 left Panonia and withdrew to the Franc king Dagobert in Bavaria. Nobody knew why after offering them a warm welcome , Dagobert gave orders to his people to kill the Bulgarians. The survived 700 families managed to draw off by fighting. They crossed the Alps and arrived in Langobardy were many of their compatriots had already lived. At last, they were well received and accommodated at first in the region of Venice and after 668 AD-in the deserted coastal regions of Ravena Exarchate- the present

Italian region of Campobasso. Two hundred years later, one ancient writer, known as Paul the Deacon, visited them. They spoke Latin and Bulgarian. Naturally the Italian people had assimilated them in the course of time. But even nowadays some localities in the regions of Rimini and Osimo are named "the Bulgarian land", "the Bulgarian place" or "the land of the Bulgarian baron" etc.

Gravestone inscription of the parents of the Bulgarian tsar Samuil (997–1018), Xth C. AD

Stone inscription from Pliska VIIIth C. AD

The church of the monastery "St. Haum", built by Tsar Boris I in 900

Stone column with carved inscription, containing treaty between Bulgaria and Byzantium signed in 815

Way of Life, Economy, Culture, and Social System of the Bulgarians until the Foundation of the Bulgarian State

Chapter IV

Apparently, when a period of nearly 700 years is studied, all events may be presented in progress. And the development that the Bulgarians had undergone over a 700-year span was really incredible. They got rapidly ahead of peoples, with which they had had an equal start before, in the Afghan valleys. They left behind including their cousins-the Avarians, Pecheneges, Koumanians and Uzians.

Without doubt, the Bulgarians were nomads in their homeland. It does not mean, as many people believe wrongly, that they used to live on horse and carts always on the move to somewhere. The nomadic way of living as a scientific term, means a method of production applied by the peoples whose main occupation is the cattle breeding. The nomads also, inhabited permanent settlements where they used to spend only the winters. During the remain-

Miniature representing a feast of the Bulgarian Khan Krum (801–814) in Bulgarian manuscript from 1345

ing three seasons the men and the grown-up children continuously moved with their herds across all over tribe's territories in search for pasture. Those, who had been engaged in cattle breeding in the Bulgarian lands kept on practising the same way until the Balkan Wars. The women from the towns of Kotel and Geravna, as it was known, might have hardly been able to see their husbands and their nearly grown-up boys except during the time span from Christmas to the end of February. The rest time they and their herds were in Dobrudja together. It was the same in Smoljan, Shiroka Luka, Dospat. The men from those towns and their sheep used to lead together a nomadic way of life in the Mediterranean Thrace .

Even though the nomadic way of life had spread over 100% of the Altaian population, this percent decreased in their new living places in

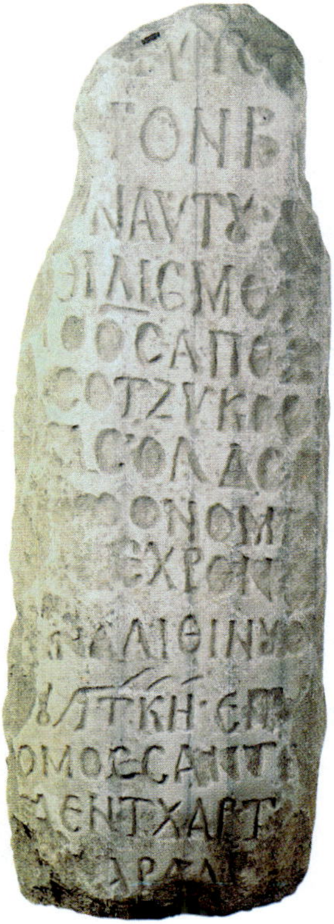

Fragment from stone column with inscription, Pliska, VIIIth C. AD

Fortress walls and entrance to the medieval Bulgarian capital, Preslav (893–971)

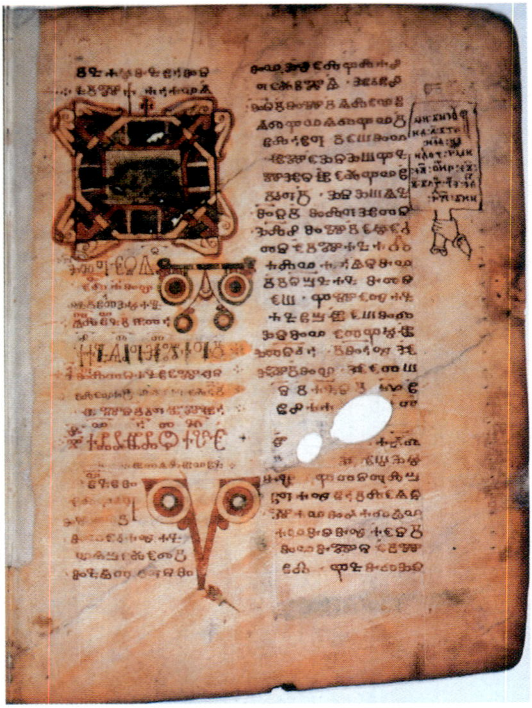

Sheet of Assemanius' gospel, Glagolitic alphabet, IXth C. AD

the North Black Sea's valley and Crimea. The Bulgarians who had settled in there for 300 years, constructed big cities and fortresses and persistently developed mining industry and metallurgy. They needed considerable quantities of metal to produce weapons and agrarian tools. Yes, even for agrarian tools. The archaeological excavations had proved unambiguously that not small part of the Bulgarian population started land cultivating, sowing and reaping. Moreover, some seeds discovered in excavations proved centuries-long selection work, whose objectives had been to obtain high-quality sorts.

The Bulgarian achievements at that age astonished even their

Medieval basilica "The Ancient bishopric" in Nesebur, VI–XIVth C. AD

contemporaries. The amazed Armenian historians wrote that the Bulgarians were the only ones to possess stone towns north of Caucasus, while all the other tribes were living in huts, tents and dugouts. The metal extraction enabled them to arm and cover with armour their warriors as well as their horses. Some skills and achievement of the Bulgarian medicine men (difficult skull operations) and mathematicians (amazingly precise calendar), are highly admired even nowadays by the relevant specialists.

Naturally, the economic and technological Bulgarian progress, in comparison with other barbaric peoples was due neither to their racial superiority nor to being among the God's elect. Both in the past and these days, there were peoples, which had closed inside themselves by rejecting everything coming from outside. In the same time, there were peoples, which had eagerly accepted and developed further the others' ideas, cultures and technologies. The Bulgarians apparently belonged to the second type. Besides everything else, they had the chance to live by the borders of the great world's civilisations-China, India, Persia and Byzantium from whom they drew on willingly everything useful in each field of life.

It is difficult to say something about their racial type from IVth. AD onwards. A widespread general vision captured the imagination of

St Clement – Bulgarian enlightener from Xth C., statue in Ohrid

The Ohrid Lake

The patriarchal church "St. Sofia" in Ohrid, built by Tsar Boris I in 865

The monastery "St. Naum", Ohrid, the beginning of Xth C. AD

the Bulgarian average contemporary. It envisages them as short curved-legged mongoloids (even the Byzantines, who have not loved them have not written anything about such racial type). This vision has not been confirmed neither by the ancient sources of information nor by the archaeological excavations. Even the ancient writer have mentioned them as tall, slender and extremely strong people. An Arabian geographer even complained that ten Arabs were not capable to fight with one Bulgarian. The archaeological excavations of the Bulgarian necropolis dating from VII–IXth. C. in Pliska, Kjulevtcha, Novi Pazar etc. showed that the average height of the buried Bulgarians was 1.75 (five feet ten). At that time the average height of the Europeans was 1.60 (five feet four).

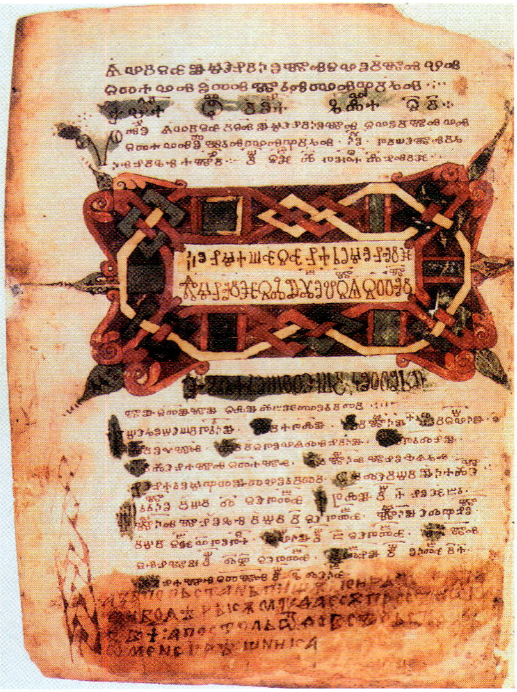

Title-page of the Assemanius' gospel, preserved in Vatikan, written in Glagolitic alphabet invented by Cyril and Methodius IXth C. AD

There is anything unusual in both the physical strength and height of the Bulgarians. It has been proven long before, that the height is in direct proportion to meat consuming and body training. The large number of high-productive herds provides a lot of meat for the Bulgarian menu; the military service and hard work in field give them the physical training.

The Iranians, as known, were not mongoloids as well. It was quite doubtful though that even the Iranian racial type had survived after the three centuries long settled life between the Caucasus, the Black and Caspian Seas. The extremely open and tolerant social system discussed hereinafter attracted many people from other peoples, who had been driven out or escaped on their own for various reasons. The Bulgarians assimilated thousands of Sarmatians and Scythians on the Black Sea littoral. They kidnapped tens of thousands men, women, Slavs, Thracian, Romans, Greeks during each one of their numerous campaigns to Central Europe and to South of the Danube, who were all gradually integrated into the Bulgarian society later without any ves-

Gravestone inscription of Mostich-high state official in IX–Xth C. AD, written in Cyrilic alphabet

Lead seal of Boris I (852–889)

Golden pectoral icon-reliquary,
Xth C. AD

tige of discrimination. Therefore, it is impossible to talk about typical Bulgarian racial type, which may have existed during the time of the founder of the Bulgarian Kingdom Khan Kubrat. According to some linguists the name "Bulgar" means "mixture" or alloy of different people from different peoples.

The religion of the Bulgarian back in their homeland was animistic. The cult of ancestors, traditional medical practices shamanism and believes in the main God-Tangra infused inside each other. However, a noticeable religious tolerance reigned over society.

Both, the archaeological excavations and written sources testified that there were Christians, Buddhists and Judaics amongst the Bulgarians, who had inhabited the Black Sea Shore. Christian was, as we would see, even the founder of the present Bulgarian state-khan Kubrat. Other khans ruling during the pagan period were Christians as well.

The Bulgarian military science deserved a special attention. The army consisted of all the men, physically healthy and fit for military service. In moment of terrible ordeals young women were recruited as well. The contemporary reminiscence in the Bulgarian society claims: one man who has not been a soldier is not a real man. Probably this sentence has remained from that time. Severe common law, which was substituted later for legislature, regulated the rights and obligations of the members of the armed forces. Even their statutes were to some extent, close in meaning to the contemporary army's regulations. The mounted troops were prevailing in army. Besides the traditional for the steppe's peoples light cavalry, the Bulgarians had heavy-armed squads of warriors whose bodies and horses were covered with metal or felt armours. The blow of the heavy-armed cavalry (at the age of Krum-the beginning of IX C.– it counted 30 000 warriors) caused such effect, which could be equal today to an attack of tank army on infantry divisions just armed with light small firearms. Actually, the permanent Bulgarian victories over Byzantium were due mostly to stunning blows inflicted by the heavy cavalry. The heavy-armed horsemen had not ever exceeded 400 in the Byzantine army.

Weaponry of the Bulgarians consisted of sabres, battle axes, knives, spears (for the heavy cavalry), lances and bows. Supported by their armies, the Bulgarians survived the turmoil of the Great Migration of Peoples and lived long enough to have their moment of glory.

Golden discus, discovered in the Bulgarian medieval capital (between 893–971), Preslav, Xth C. AD

Golden pectoral icon-reliquary, Xth C. AD

Ceramic altar, discovered in the Bulgarian capital Preslav, Xth C. AD

Khan Kubrat and the Birth of Bulgaria

Chapter V

Pectoral icon with two saints, bone, Preslav, Xth C. AD

The idea that in the middle of VIth. C. the Bulgarians, inhabiting the area situated between Caucasus, the Black and the Caspian Seas were subjugated and were conquered by the Turkic Khanate, has persistently captured the mind of the contemporary Bulgarian. It is not quite correct and truthfully especially regarding the contemporary terms "subjugated" and "joke. At that time the relations between the ancient peoples and their rulers have specific features, which could not be get into the parameters of the contemporary notions.

The truth was, that in 567–568 khagan Silgibu-the main ruler of the so-called Turkic Khanate (formation of state type, born in Altai by the merger of many Turkic tribes were no one was superior) forced the Bulgarians, the Khazars and the

Belengers to join this Turkic Empire. The specific character of this state formation excludes the term "joke" of the Bulgarians. The Bulgarian tribal leaders were not assassinated but continued to rule over their tribes. Moreover, probably they were united for the first time. Because the Turkic Khanate, as it was known, even being ruled by one ruler, was divided into eight semi-self-governing parts, governed by deputies chosen out of their prevailing population's background. Gostun, mentioned in the List of the Bulgarian Khans, was such a deputy. Apparently as early as 581, the khanate fell apart into southern and eastern parts as a result of the internecine struggles for the throne. The Bulgarians, who had remained in the Western Khanate probably were majority, or gradually became majority of its population, and their chiefs started taking part in the struggles for the supreme power. Obviously, they did not succeed, just like their brothers in the Avarian Khanate, but they acted much more wisely. They unified in 632 around the person of Kubrat, who was the chief of one of the tribes that had left the khanate and founded a kingdom. The Byzantine authors, contemporaries of those events, wrote about a kingdom. They even called it

Golden necklace, discovered in the Bulgarian capital Preslav, Xth C. AD

Bronze reliquary-cross, Xth C. AD

"Great" one. Obviously they had noticed by observing it all typical features of state activity as: boundaries, territory, economy, state structures, independent centralised government and legislature. All these features made them different from those alliances of tribes, which united temporarily in order to attack and rob some Byzantine province or from another tribe that enriched its self by robbery.

Unfortunately, the Byzantine sources were not verbose at all, when the word went on the first leader of the Bulgarian State.

The earliest Bulgarian chronicle-The List of the Bulgarian Khans-reported to us, that he had originated from the Dulo family. The chronicle of the Byzantine patriarch Nicephorus, who had lived hundreds of years after, messaged that he was nephew of Organa. Without doubt, Organa was an important person. However, the ancients knew who he was but they did not tell us. We could logically presume that he was deputy of this part of the West Turkic Khanate, which the Bulgarian tribes were included in.

It is difficult to specify birth date of Kubrat-the first head of the Bulgarian State. According to another Byzantine writer's message, who had written about him, we learned that Kubrat was dispatched to Constantinople since he was a child for unknown reasons. He grew up in the emperor's palace, where he adopted the Christianity. The historians presume after comparing the scanty pieces of information that khan Kubrat lives in Constantinople between 610–632. The uncertainty surrounding the reasons, for which he has been dispatched to the capital of the Roman Empire does not have also endless parameters.

Bronze reliquary-cross, IXth C. AD

Actually, the possibilities were two. He was a hostage, or he was sent there in order to study. As Simeon was sent quarter of millennium later for the second reason. Kubrat could not have been a hostage, because the Bulgarian tribes had not already existed independently and it was not up to them to decide whether to make war with Byzantium or not. If Byzantium had been in any position to require hostages from the West Turkic Khanate, it would have asked its ruler's son. Therefore, the assumption that Kubrat had been sent by his famous uncle in order to study was the only one remaining possibility.

Silver repoussee cover of a gospel with image of the Bulgarian man of letters "St. Clement", silver with gilt, XIVth C. AD

Twenty-two years in Constantinople-the capital of the European civilisation at that epoch and centuries later-could be spent in a different way. One person could indulge in good time and easy life. Both, the Constantinople's pubs and free manners especially (and mostly) of the women with aristocratic background were famous.

Despite the lack of any information, we should hardly have any doubt that Kubrat took advantage of the high education, which he had got in order to take in both culture and state formation experience. It seemes to me that nobody has yet taken in the fact that he studies and spends much more time in Constantinople than Simeon the Great and Kalojan did it.

Crown of the Bulgarian archbishop in Ohrid, gold, XVIIth C. AD

Novelists or movie-makers, who quite often represent him as a primitive steppe leader, with dirty felt hair and manners of a peasant elder, must know that khan Kubrat proba-

Stone statue of the blessing Christ, discovered in Nessebur, XIth C. AD

bly has been one of the highest educated people in Europe at this time. All his further activities prove this statement.

So, according to the testimony of the Byzantine chroniclers, khan Kubrat took advantage of the weakness of Turkic Khanate in 632,overthrew the vassalage of his tribe and declared himself independent ruler. All the Bulgarian tribes from the areas along the Black, Azovian and Caspian Seas joined him with the speed of lightning. The new-born state formation was not a tribal military alliance (such juridical categories did not exist in the past), but a state. It was state, which had precisely fixed territory, state administration of its own, laws treating equally all the subjects (on the base probably of the common law of the Bulgarian tribes) and its own foreign policy. Both the Bulgarian monuments of the time and Byzantium considered it as a state. The statesmen and chroniclers of the latter called it "Bulgaria", or even "The Great Bulgaria". Therefore, since then, the names of the Bulgarian tribes disappeared forever from the pages written by the ancient chroniclers, who begun to call them just "Bulgarians".

There were no pieces of information about some Turkcic counteraction to khan Kubrat's campaign. Obviously the Khanate had not any military capabilities to take the Bulgarian tribes-separatists back to the state. Actually, the Khazars would split off in the same way.

The scanty data, which came through the Byzantine and Armenian chroniclers, gave us the opportunity to define even with some doubts, the frontiers of "Great Bulgaria". In the west it was lying along the lower course of the Danube, in the south- along the Black and Azovian Seas, in the east- the Kuban River and in north-the Donets River. According to some assumptions the capital of Bulgaria was the present town

Ruins of the so-called Golden church, built in the Bulgarian capital Preslav by tsar Simeon the Great between 893–927

Fanagoria, which was situated on the Azovian Sea Coast.

As we saw, in Byzantium, Khan Kubrat acquired formidable knowledge of construction and functioning of the state system. He, beyond any doubt, persisted in introducing perfectly functioning administration to the new-born state in conformity with the Bulgarian standards and tradition. The state was governed by a khan, who took the decisions after having discussed them with the Council of the Great Boyls. The kavkhan was his assistant (substitute) and second person in the administrative hierarchy. The ichirgu-boil took the third place. They were at the same time, high state officials and high officers in the army, in command of huge military formations in wartime. Combining the adminis-

The Church in "St. Panteleimon" monastery in Ohrid, build in 887 by tsar Boris, the regional governor Dometa and St. Clement

trative power with the military functions was typical practice of all the other levels in hierarchy.

Unfortunately, the ancient written sources offered quite scanty information concerning the internal development and interstate relations of Bulgaria at Kubrat's age. As a Christian, Byzantine alumnus and close personal friend to emperor Iraclius, he managed to keep peaceful relations and good neighbourhood with the empire to the end of his rule. In 635, those wonderful relations were regulated by international treaty, which came as an indirect act of recognition of the new state. Khan Kubrat was honoured with the title "patricius". Some events after his death made us believe that his friendship with

The church of "St. Panteleimon",Ohrid, IXth C. AD, keeping the relics of the ancient Bulgarian writer St. Clement, died in 916

Ohrid-capital of Medieval Bulgaria between 997–1018; seat of the Bulgarian Patriarchy and autocephalous archbishopric between 997–1767

emperor Iraclius had occurred in purely human terms. After Iraclius' death in 642, khan Kubrat supported his widow Martina and her children, to whom he had been very devoted, in their struggle for the emperor's

throne even with risk to spoil the relations with Byzantium.

According to the European chronicler John of Nikius, both the people and army revolted led by someone Jutalius, son of Constantine, as quick as they heart the announcement that Kubrat had supported Martina and her children. The information of John of Nikius also testified that khan Kubrat had conflicts with the "barbaric tribes" along the frontier, but his troops always won thanks to the fact that he was Christian. Perhaps the harsh conflict with the khazars started since that moment onwards. After Kubrat's death, they took over the eastern state territory, forced Asparukh to look for territorial enlargement and made him to move the capital to the south of the Danube.

The war with the Khazars' State, whose history was traced by the sources, was an event, which became for the second and last time reason for recording the interstate relations of Bulgaria from Kubrat's

The fortress of Bulgarian tsar Samuil (997–1018) in Ohrid

Ruins of the palace of Bulgarian tsars in Preslav (893–971)

Tower in the Shumen fortress, Xth C. AD

Title-page of Bulgarian manuscript, XIVth C. AD

time. The other neighbour peoples were too bad organised to be capable to measure their strength with the Bulgarians or to make any claims on them. The Khazars' Kingdom, which had been founded on the Caspian Sea North Coast, declared itself successor of the Turkic Khanate. On this base, it made claims over all its former lands and tribes eastwards. However, it was they to make up the territory and the population of Bulgaria.

So, the conflict was unavoidable. Unfortu-nately, its vicissitudes remained unknown. However, the indirect information, as we had seen above, pointed out that the attacks were overthrown successfully at least till Kubrat's death. If we peered more carefully into the text of a medieval legend, which had been thought to be example for statesman wisdom, we would find out that it contained information about the attitudes in the Bulgarian society that had appeared as a result of the long-year war with the Khazars. We were speaking of the legend reported by a Byzantine chronicler telling us that khan Kubrat, already on his deathbed, called his sons and made a request to them to break a bundle of dry vine sticks. No one managed to do it. Afterwards Khan Kubrat broke all the sticks one by one with his feeble old man's hands. The lesson became quite clear. Bulgaria would be invincible until the Bulgarians and their political leaders were united. If they let disunity prevail over society and their actions, both they and Bulgaria would be one by one destroyed.

Icon "Archangels", XVth C. AD

Serious suspicions and anxieties motivated khan Kubrat's determination to give this lesson to his closest associates. They were caused by some tendencies in the Bulgarian political leadership, which had been provoked by the Khazars' invasion. And they were really reasonable. The numerous casualties and crucial economic losses were the price of the successful opposition to the Khazars' raids. All the Bulgarian lands were flat and without natural shelters and became easy prey for the Khazar mounted squads. They had probably pilled, set on fire and robbed tens of villages until the Bulgarian troops finally found and destroyed them. Many Bulgarians were aware that the Bulgarian territory was situated just on the Great road of the peoples coming from Asia and Europe and as if the Khazars attacking Bulgaria were completely destroyed their place would be taken by other people with the speed of lightning. If the events were assessed by what hap-

Reliquary,
XVIIIth C. AD

pened after Kubrat's death, some of the Bulgarians and, precisely speaking, their political leaders insisted that the state should be protected exactly within the current borders of its territories. Obviously Kubrat was one of them and his authority and strength stopped the people who disagreed with his policy. After having seen the lack of perspective in keeping those territories, they obviously insisted on fighting for new lands, which would have natural protective lines, mineral wealth and better climate. However, they obviously were divided in their statement as well. Ones of them insisted on seeking for those lands far from the Peoples' route and avoiding in general the neighbourhood of strong state formations. The others insisted just on the quality of the new lands without being afraid of potential enemies of their own domain. The circumstances after Kubrat's death – some of the Bulgarians went northward and founded a new state ; the others expanded the Bulgarian territories further south of the Danube, where they had moved their capital after – proved that there were such tendencies.

Kubrat died in 651. Fanagoria was thought to be the place of his death. However, the new interpretation of one sumptuous burial made by Joahim Werner showed that the death caught him hundreds of kilometres northwards in the present Ukrainian steppes. It allowed us to have a closer look at Kubrat last statesman's efforts. It is worth telling the story about the Bulgarian ruler's end and his grave.

In 1912 an exceptionally rich burial was found near the Ukrainian village Malaja Pereshchepina, 13 kilometres from the town of Poltava in the sand dunes of Vorskila River. The defunct was buried in wooden coffin plated with 250 rectangular golden plates whose size was 6,5x5,5 centimetres. A considerable quantity of precious-metal vessels were laid beside him- (20 silver and 17 golden), plus weapons incrusted with precious metal, signs of power-a golden corn and a golden spoon, 69 golden coins, nearly half-a-kilo golden buckle, golden rings etc. It made even the first researchers to define this tomb not just as last shelter of some wealthy man or noble commander, but as last shelter of the state's head of some of the barbaric state formations, which had ruled over those lands for a long (or short) time.

The vessels were not of special importance for the precise treasure's dating, because they had been gathered in the course of at least two centuries. However, the latest coins (of the Byzantine emperor Constantine II) dated from 647-unambiguous indication that the funeral was held after that date. Some of the vessels, related to the Christian cult, pointed out that the buried man was a Christian.

The church "St. John Theologian" (Kaneo), Ohrid, XI–XIIth C. AD

The church "St. Virgin Mary Perivlepta" ("St. Clement"), Ohrid, XIth C. AD. Seat of the Bulgarian autocephalous archbishopric in XV–XVIIIth C. AD

Reliquary of St. Dionissius, silver with gilt, XVIIIth C. AD

Even these facts were enough to prove that Khan Kubrat was the only one to correspond to the archaeological evidences of Malaja Pereshchepina burial, amongst all the possible persons, who had ruled over tribes or states at that age. In 1983 d-r W. Zeibt from the Institute of Byzantine Studies in Vienna succeeded in deciphering the monograms on both golden rings-seals as "Hubratu" and "Hubratu patrikiu". There was no longer doubt that the Russian archaeologists discovered in 1912 the grave of the founder of Great Bulgaria.

The burial place, which was situated on the last north country's point, hundreds of kilometres from the capital, put in absolutely different light the last days of life of the great Bulgarian. He obviously did not finish his life exhausted by illness and old age (actually, if he was a child in 610, then in 651 the khan was 55–60 years old-a man at the height of his power). He probably headed the victorious opposition of his troops to the new Khazar's incursion, which was this time met and smashed just at the frontier. The particular burial testified that the Khazars were really defeated and thrown out. The specially made expensive coffin, the expensive grave offerings, as well as the strict observing of rite, revealed that the funeral was held in a relaxed atmosphere. If defeated, the khan would not have had even a grave.

Miniature from medieval Bulgarian Psalter, 1360

But how has the Bulgarian ruler died? Visited by a treacherous disease during the military campaign, or dead from his wounds after the victorious fight? We do not know, but it does not matter. Khan Kubrat has died protecting Bulgaria.

And something else arouses bewilderment. Why has his corps not been brought to the capital and buried there with the same honours; and why has his tumulus been built just at the frontier? It seemes that before closing his eyes forever, Kubrat has had enough time to oblige his commanders to bury him just at the frontier. In this way, he turns his grave into defender of Bulgaria, because the cult of ancestors has been too strictly observed by the Bulgarians. No one enemy could tread their lands without being unpunished. Thus, khan Kubrat put his descendants under the obligation, even through his

Medieval Bulgarian church in the village of Kalishte near Struga, XII–XIIIth C. AD

Icon "St. George", XVIIIth C. AD

tomb, to defend to death the borders of Bulgaria.

Khan Asparukh-Expansion of the Bulgarian State South of the Danube

Chapter VI

After Khan Kubrat's death the Khazars attacked Bulgaria further. They managed to take over the Bulgarian territories in the Caucasian region, the river valleys of the Kuban and the Don, as well as the Crimean Peninsula. Some of the Bulgarian tribes accepted their dependence on the Khazars. Others withdrew far northward to the Kama and Volga river valleys, where they founded a big Bulgarian state. The so-called Volgo-Kama Bulgaria existed until XIII Th C., when it vanished under the Tartars' blows. Nowadays, many peoples declare themselves descendants of that Bulgarians-Chuvashes, Balkars, Kazan's Tartars, Turkestanians and others from both the Russian

Federation and states in Central Asia. There is even a powerful movement named "Bulgarian National Congress" in Tatarstan (whose members substitute the nationality in their passports for "Nationality-Bulgarian"). Khan Asparukh, the descendent of Kubrat, was already ruling only over the territory between the Dnepre, the Danube and the Donets in the early seventies of VIIth C. After desperate defensive battles he

Fragment from mural painting in Urvich fortress, XIIIth C. AD

Icon "St. Virgin Mary", mosaic, XIVth C. AD

Mural painting from the rock church in the village of Ivanovo, XIVth C. AD

managed to drive the Khazars back to the other riverside of the Dnepre and stopped their offensive westwards by inflicting them stunning blows.

However, Khan Asparukh was aware of being unable to provide worthwhile life for his people and state on the only one surviving piece of Bulgaria-infertile valleys, swampy areas with no natural shelters ore deposits and forests. Therefore, the Bulgarian statesmen decided in their turn to undertake territorial expansion and to occupy the lands of ancient Moesia. According to the

Icon of "St. Virgin Mary" from Nessebur, XIII–XIVth C. AD

Byzantine authors they liked this land, because the deep-flowing Danube protected it in the north, the stone wall of the Balkan Range protected it in the south and the Black Sea did it in the east.

At that time, Moesia, as well as the whole peninsula had already been inhabited for a century by numerous Slavic tribes that had assimilated the former population. The Byzantine Empire, engaged in crippling wars in VI–VIIth C. with the Persians and Arabs, had fully lost its control on its European domains. However since the mid of VIIth C. Byzantium started its re-conquest on the Balkans after getting rid of his troubles in Asia Minor. The disunited Slavic tribes in Greece, Albania, Macedonia, and Thrace were subjugated to the imperial power. Seven Slavic tribes inhabiting Moesia formed a military and political alliance, whose objectives were to oppose to the Byzantine re-conquest. But its chances to counteract efficiently to the mighty empire were minimal. The Slavic troops were only consisted of lightly armed infantrymen.

In 680, khan Asparukh transferred considerable part of the Bulgarian army and population to the south of the Danube delta and occupied the present Dobrudja's lands. As a matter of fact, this act meant declaring war on the Byzantine Empire. The common interests of both the Bulgarians and Slavs, who were equally threatened by Byzantium, made them to conclude a treaty under which the Slavic tribes in Moesia recognised its dependence on the Bulgarian state, which on its part, accepted the obligation to protect its subjects from any enemy's attacks.

In the war between Bulgaria and Byzantium in 680, both the Bulgarian cavalry and Slavic infantry divisions inflicted to the Byzantine troops, which were led personally by emperor Constantine IV Pogonatus, series of consecutive

Title-page of Bulgarian manuscript, XIVth C. AD

Miniature from medieval Bulgarian manuscript, XVIth C. AD

stunning blows. The battlefield moved to Thrace. While the capital city of Pliska- the new administrative and political centre- was being under construction in the northern part of Moesia, the rumble of the Bulgarian mounted regiments reverberated more and more often over the hills along the Bosporus. In the autumn of 681, Byzantium was forced to conclude a peace treaty with Bulgaria as well as to recognise both the detachment of Moesia from the empire and Slavic-Bulgarian agreement.

Some changes were made in the Bulgarian State's structure in compliance with the treaty of Khan Asparukh with the Slavic princes of Moesia. The supreme power belonged to the Bulgarian aristocracy. It was some kind of recognition of its merits in the struggles against the external state's enemy and recognition of the real military force, which supported it. The khan, whose power was hereditary and the council of the Twelve great boyls (representatives of the noble families) headed the state. It was some kind of particular government. Each one of the Great boyls was responsible for definite scope of activities such as: foreign policy, economics, and etc. The decisions of paramount importance for the state had been taken by the so-called people assembly -meeting of the representatives of all the noble Bulgarian families plus the princes of the Slavic tribes included in the Bulgarian State. The Slavic tribes retained their internal self-governing and the territories, as specified by the treaty from 680. Their obligations to the Bulgarian State were to pay definite taxes to the central government and to participate with military formations in state defence.

Khan Kuber– Foundation of the Second Bulgarian State in Macedonia

Chapter VII

According to one Byzantine source ("The miracles of Saint Dimitris"), in 680, about 60 000 Bulgarians led by Khan Kuber, who had inhabited the present Hungarian lands, then situated within the boundaries of the Avarian state, tried to take over the supreme state power through revolt. After their failure, they crossed the Danube and settled in the present Bitolja field after following the route Belgrade-Nish-Scopjie-Prilep. At this place, their Khan Kuber, founded a small Bulgarian state. One year later, he tried to take the city of Thessalonica, where he intended to establish the capital of his state. After the failure of that operation, Khan Kuber obviously launched his conquest to other directions. In 688, Kuber and khan Asparukh's Danube Bulgaria participated together in a war against Byzantium. There was no information in the medieval chronicles about the development of this state. However, the archaeological monuments discovered by Albanian and Yugoslavian archaeologists pointed out, that Khan Kuber's Bulgaria gradually occupied the already abandoned by Byzantium (in VIth C.) fields situated by Ressen, Okhrid, Korcha, Kichevo, Tetovo, Skopjie and Kossova. According to some inscriptions on the Madara horseman's relief situated in present Northern Bulgaria, the state founded by Kuber kept

Shroud with image of St. Virgin Mary, 1230

on being in touch with the Danube Bulgaria in VIIIth. C., although it had been made detached from it by the Byzantine domains. The present Western Bulgaria and Eastern Macedonia were constituent parts of those Byzantine territories. Apparently several attempts to break trough that dividing line were made. Massive military divisions were sent to that direction in 792 and 807, but they could not break trough the Byzantine defence. However, in 811–812, Khan Krum's troops took over those territories. A direct contact was established between both Bulgarian states and they finally merged into one state.

Mural painting of "St. Ilia in the cave" from the church "Forty Holy Martyrs" in Tarnovo, XIVth C. AD

Miniature from Bulgarian manuscript, XIVth C. AD

The Bulgarian State-Guard of Europe in the Early Middle Ages

Chapter VIII

The appearance of Bulgaria – a stable, civilised and military powerful state in the European east, had incredibly beneficial consequences for the European civilisation. Even because its armies stopped the barbaric waves coming from Asia, periodically rushing into West Europe and devastating both its economy and population. And there, they took in by themselves very soon that the Bulgarians were good fighters. It was truth that Bulgaria and Byzantum had problems quite often, but they did not concern anything but solely the domination over the Balkan territories populated by the Slavs. The Bulgarian political thought had not ever aimed to destroy completely Byzantium or to add to its own territories areas inhabited by non-Slavic population. Besides, thirty or forty-year spells, even half-a-century-long peace periods succeeded usually the short-lasted military conflicts. It allowed Byzantium-the successor of the antique European civilisation-to survive eight centuries further, to preserve the achievements of the ancient cultural and technological heritage and to hand it over to Europe trough the transmission named Bulgaria.

We would like to remind the Europeans, who knew that Charles Martell rescued the Old Continent in VIIIth C. from the first Islamic aggression in the battle of Poitier in 732, that the Arabic invasion at that time was going simultaneously through

Icon "St. Virgin Mary and St. John Theologian", v. Poganovo, XIVth C. AD

Page from medieval Bulgarian manuscript, XVth C. AD

both European entrances-the Gibraltar and Bosporus. And, as if the Arabs had finally succeeded in squeezing trough the Gibraltar and holding for a long time the Iberian Peninsula, before in 732 Charles Martell stopped them in Poitie, the Bulgarians ruthlessly defeated them along the Bosporus, threw them out of Europe and pushed them deep into Asia for a long time. They did it despite the fact that the Arabic military forces that attacked Europe on this point were much stronger than those, which attacked through the Gibraltar. Charles Martell and his 7000 Franc soldiers fought against 6000 Arabic soldiers, meanwhile the Bulgarians had to cope with 100 000 Arabic invaders.

The events were worth being described. Many Arabic, Greek, Latin and Ancient-Bulgarian authors-contemporaries of those battles left many testimonies. In 717, an Arabic army of ten thousand soldiers was transferred to Europe and besieged Constantinople, after defeating the Byzantine troops in Asia Minor. The city was tightly surrounded, running out of supplies and starved. Its downfall appeared to be inevitable.

Suddenly, the Bulgarian army emerged on the hills in front of the Arabic camp. The citizens of Constanti-nople got embarrassed at first. They were not looking for help from the Bulga-rians, with whom they had waged war for a Slavic region one year before. They thought that the Bulgarians would take advantage of their difficult position to make alliance with the Arabs and to put an end to the empire. However, when the Bulgarians slaughtered under their eyes some drifting out of the camp Arabic squads, they got persuaded that the unexpected ally had come.

Obviously, the Bulgarian intervention was not motivated by wish for territorial expansion. The Bulgarians withdrew after the events without any compensation claims. Obviously their opposition to the Arabs was due to the appearing awareness of affiliation to one community. It was the community of the European Christian Civilisa-tion, whose worthies and values were threatened by a mighty enemy, who had not anything in common with them. Although Christianity was not yet an official religion, it was professed by large part of the population as well as by the Bulgarian ruler Khan Tervel. Therefore, in this case the often-repeated acts of hostility were forgotten in the name of general survival of the Christians.

The Arabic troops, even in a crossfire (between the Constan-tinople's garrison and the Bulgarian army), were considerably more numerous than both the Bulgarians and Byzantine allied troops taken together. But their commanders did not dare to meet the Bulgarians in decisive battle. Although the Arabs were perfect fighters they had no available armed horsemen unlike the Bulgarian army in which their number was about 30 000. Therefore, they drew back to their camp that encircled the whole Constantinople and continued the siege.

But the situation had already changed. The recovered Byzantine fleet got out of the Bosporus and defeated in several combats the Arabic one. In this way it provided the transportation of foods to Constantinople and stopped the carriage of food supply, at least by sea, to the Arabic camp.

Page from medieval Bulgarian manuscript, XVIth C. AD

The Bulgarians took care of it on the ground. The Arabic ration squads were killed not far than a mile from the camp by the light Bulgarian cavalry. At that moment, starvation burst out in the Arabic camp.

Nevertheless, the Arabs stand a whole year. In the summer of 718, their army

The medieval Bulgarian town of Shumen, VII–XIVth C. AD

Fortress walls of the medieval Bulgarian town of Shumen, VII–XIVth C. AD

The church "St. John Precursor" in Nessebur, Xth C. AD

squeezed out of the camp and drew up in battle order in front of the Bulgarians. Apparently it was a desperate attempt. The Arabic generals knew that they had no chance against the situated near Constantinople's hills Bulgarian army, which had had a dull time for a whole year. The Arabic cavalry, which first attacked, was really smashed in minutes by the armed Bulgarian horses and warriors. The Franc authors gave different number for the killed by the Bulgarians Arabs. Zigibertus wrote that "the Bulgarians killed 30 000 Saracens". The monk Alberick evaluated the Arabic casualties to 32 000. The number of casualties in this case was not so important as the fact that the Arabic invasion of Europe was over. The Arabs were not just thrown out of Europe, but also persecuted, beaten and driven by both the Bulgarian and Byzantine squads to Asia Minor near the pre-conflict Byzantine boundaries. In this way, a Christian barrier that would stay long centuries further was raised in front of the Islam. Hardly the second aggression of Islam would be conducted during XIV–XVth C. This time it would be led by the Ottoman Turks and would cause the rout both of Bulgaria and Byzantium, which could not succeeded in uniting their efforts against the common enemy, as they did it in VIIIth C. The lack of support to the Christian East from Western Europe would drive the Islam to the walls of Vienna, Venice and Warsaw. But this is already another theme.

The church "St. Dimitar", built in 1185 in the Bulgarian capital Tarnovo

Tzarevetz-the fortified aristocratic quarter in the Bulgarian capital Tarnovo (1185–1393)

The medieval church "St. Peter and Paul" in the Bulgarian capital (between 1185–1393), Tarnovo

The Bulgarian Idea about the National State – Base of the European Civilisation

Chapter IX

The appearance of the first Slavic state in Europe and the increasing of its power turned it inevitably into an unifying centre of the Slavs in Southeast and Central Europe. Those Slavic tribes, which had lost their independence and had been included in the territories of non-Slavic state formations – Eastern and Western Roman Empire and the Avarian Khanate, gravitated particularly strong to Bulgaria.

Ryphidion-silver with gilt and enamel, XVIIth C. AD

Ryphidion-silver with gilt and enamel, XVIth C. AD

During VII–IXth the cases of separatism of several regions inhabited by the Slavs and their incorporation to Bulgaria were fairly common phenomenon. As a result, Bulgaria continuously enlarged its territories. In the mid of IXth C. Bulgaria turned out to be huge Slavic empire, whose borders stretched from the present areas in Eastern Austria as far as the Don River and from the Krakow region in Poland to the Aegean Sea Coast.

After securing peace in Western Europe by stopping the barbaric invasions, the Bulgarian political thought said the last word on the main question concerning the Old Continent at that age- the way of its development.

There were two possibilities. The first was the foundation of unified European State. In practical aspect the idea meant restoration of the Roman Empire. Naturally, Christianity would be the ideological basis of this super-state. The Greek or Latin should be the languages of its population. Christi-anity gave the arguments of this political idea "God is the only one in heaven, one is the God's realm"-its apologists asserted- "therefore, his reflection on Earth should have the same effect-one kingdom, one religion, one people, one language". In order to implement this idea, all the national states that variegated with their frontiers in 476 the European map after Roman Empire's downfall had to be destroyed. Assimilation of both, the new and old nations by the envisaged unique Greek or Roman nation was planned. However, that concept of Europe's unification has nothing in common with the contemporary concept of united Europe – Europe of the united nations and cultures.

Ryphidion-silver with gilt and enamel, XVIth C. AD

The other possibility was to preserve the right of independent existence and development of each particular European nation. It was the way, which Europe had finally decided on. The Bulgarian political though and its implementing on that European political arena had the main contribution to.

Ryphidion-silver with gilt and enamel, XVIth C. AD

At the end of VIIIth – the first half of IXth C., when the resolution of the question about the way of both the political and cultural developments of Europe was under way, the

Monstrance, made in the town of Chiprovetz, 1626

support of the major spiritual and political forces in Europe obviously predetermined the choice in favour of the universalistic concept.

In the West, it was the Roman (Franc) Empire and the Papacy. In the East, it was the Eastern Roman Empire (Byzantium) and the Universal Patriarch of Constantinople.

Actually, the historians had called them Western or Franc, Eastern or Byzantine Empires, for the sake of convenience in their scientific studies. The political leaderships of both superpowers just had called them "the Roman Empire". Their subjects were called "Romans". Those facts revealed in a clear manner their claims for political, historical and cultural heritage. Both the Constantinople patriarch and Roman pope supported firmly those claims.

In political aspect, the mighty Byzantium supported this idea in Eastern Europe. Its domains had not yet spanned over vast territories in Asia, the Balkan Peninsula and Italy. The Holy Roman Empire (Franc Kingdom) supported it in Western Europe.

At the end of VIIIth C., the universalistic idea started filling itself with concrete contents. In the East, Byzantium got back all former Roman Empire's provinces, which had been inhabited centuries before by the Slavs, except Moesia which had been constituent part of the Bulgarian state. In the West, emperor Charlemagne (Charles the Great) (768–814) took by sword and fire the whole Western Europe from its borders with the Arabs on the Pyrenean crests, to the middle course of the Danube. At the end of VIIIth C. three states practically existed in Europe. Two of them claimed to be successors "de jure" of the Roman Empire. The third one-Bulgaria– was founded on national base. For its real chance, although the two pretenders for the Roman heritage did not fight against each other, they were implacable enemies. However, in 800, this favourable circumstance was about to vanish. The envoys of both pretenders managed to arrange dynastic marriage between the empress Irina, at that time ruling over Eastern Rome, and Charlemagne. Contracting this marriage would have caused automatically the merger of the two parts of the Roman Empire and practically its complete restoration, except three provinces-Moesia, Thracia and Macedonia i.e. the territory of Bulgaria. In spite of its strong army, it was not difficult to guess what the Bulgarian destiny would have been, if the military resources of both the whole of Europe and big part of Asia had stand against Bulgaria. It would have been smashed just in weeks even on a "legal" base, because the Bulgarian State had occupied part of the Roman heritage.

But one of the further court's plots along the Bosporus threw the empress Irinea out of the throne and imposed a man instead. In that way, the merger by dynastic marriage of both parts of Empire failed at lest at that time. Nevertheless, hard times for Bulgaria were on the way. The new Byzantine emperor, the ambitious and talented Nicephorus II Genikus, decided to destroy the Bulgarian State and launched series of military campaigns against it. His failure during the first years did not shake him-the Bulgarians conquered Sofia forever in their counterattacks in 809. Our pre-

Reliquary, silver and gilt,
XVIIth C. AD

The Bulgarian tsar Ivan Alexander with his family (1331–1371), miniature from Bulgarian manuscript, 1355

sent capital was then the major Byzantine fortress on the Balkans. The horrifying Byzantine military operations continued in desperately methodical manner.

The military campaign in 811 was especially crucial. The Byzantine army of eight thousand warriors recruited from all the imperial provinces defeated the few Bulgarian divisions and even took over the Bulgarian capital Pliska. In the decisive battle on 26th of 811, the Bulgarian army headed by Khan Krum, in which even young women were had been recruited, encircled and killed the Byzantine troops to the last soldier. Emperor Nicephorus I Genikus died as well. His skull, plated with gold, was turned into a cup, with which khan Krum used to drink during the Bulgarian court's ceremonies.

The Bulgarian counterattack resulted in series of new fierce but victorious battles conducted in the south-Balkans Byzantine provinces. The last decisive battle took place near Versinikia in 813. The thirty-thousand-soldier corps of armoured Bulgarian cavalry predetermined the Bulgarians' victory. In the summer of 813, the Bulgarian troops reached the walls of Constantinople. Faithful to their prudence, the Bulgarians did not tried to destroy completely Byzantium by taking its capital Constantinople. They could have done it easily, after having totally crushed the Byzantine army near Versinikia. But it would have made them neighbours of the Muslim Arabian East and would made them to face new problems. Khan Krum was satisfied just with fixing his spear into the Constantinople fortifying fortress wall as a sign of victory. Then, he came back to Bulgaria and begun peace talks, which ended in the

The fortress of Kaliakra town on the Black Sea Coast, XIVth C. AD

Bulgarian annexation of the most fertile east Roman province Thracia. The exhausted Byzantium had not already been military threat to Bulgaria.

Then the Bulgarian military machine was able to face calmly the threat from the West. There, the Bulgarian diplomacy hardly held off Charlemagne's aspirations to the Bulgarian lands and prevented with last efforts a two-front war. Objectivity required mentioning that if Charlemagne was had not been so resentful towards Constantinople, and if he had not been determined just to watch with malicious joy at the defeat of his rival for the Roman throne, Bulgaria might have hardly survived. And Europe would have hit another road.

The church "St. John Neosveteni" in Nessebur, XIVth C. AD

So, the Bulgarian armies were transferred to the Central European State's frontiers. Prudent again, the Bulgarians suggested that the controversial issues related to the frontier, which could be a reason for eventual war, had to be resolved trough negotiations. According to both the chronicler (as well as Charlemagne's biographer) Einhard and annals of the Fulda monastery, the Bulgarian envoys arrived intending to specify "the borders and areas between the Francs and the Bulgarians". The successor of Charlemagne, Ludwig the Pious, prolonged the negotiations three whole years, despite the insistence of the Bulgarian ambassadors. It became clear to the Bulgarians that the Holy Roman Empire was not interested in precise fixing of its frontiers with Bulgaria, just because of its claims for the Roman heritage, including the whole of Bulgaria.

The son of Khan Krum,(the winner against Byzantium) Khan Omurtag, headed the Bulgarian political elite ruling the country. This time, they were determined not to try experiments with the capabilities of the Bulgarian army to respond to the accepted blow and attacked first. In 827, the

Reliquary, the Bulgarian autocephalous archbishopric in Ohrid, silver with gilt, XVIIIth C. AD

Fortress tower in Nessebur, VIth C. AD

Bulgarian Danube fleet squeezed trough the Drava and the Tissa rivers deep inside the Franc territories and landed troops, which acquired vast territories inhabited by the Slavs. The war lasted two years. Despite the efforts of Ludwig the Pious, who had even sent his son Ludwig of Germany to fight against the Bulgarians, the troops of the Holy Roman Empire were loosing battle after battle. The peace treaty was signed in 829. It envisaged the incorporation of another Roman province (Panonia, the present Hungry) into the Bulgarian State's territory. This conflict was interesting with the fact that another future big European capital-Budapest-was born from its vicissitudes. It emerged as two Bulgarian frontier fortresses-Buda and Pest, situated on both the left and right riversides of the Danube. At the beginning of IXth C. Bulgaria and the second Bulgarian State in Macedonia managed to unify. Byzantium had no strength enough to counteract. Moreover, the Bulgarians rescued it and gave it the chance to survive once again in 822, by crushing the revolt of a renegade, who had besieged Constantinople supported by the Arabic army.

The Bulgarian victory from the first half of IXth C. in the dramatic conflicts with both successors of Rome led not only to the survival of huge part of the Slavic population in South, Central and Eastern Europe, which was rescued from assimilation and consolidated within the borders of one state. The defeated states in the wars with Bulgaria, bearers and implementers of the universalistic idea about the European future, remained with no enough capable military strength to implement this idea in the only one possible way-the way of military power. The third superpower-the national state Bulgaria – appeared on the European political scene regardless of both "giants". Bulgaria, balancing skilfully between both giants, did not allow the success of further attempts to restoring Rome and implementing the Roman idea. The dissolution of the Franc Empire and the foundation of the new European States already on national basis, were not only made upon the Bulgarian model, but also often

Church in the town of Nessebur,XVIIth C. AD

under the direct protection (mostly in Southeast Europe) of the powerful at that time Bulgarian Kingdom. The contradictions between the three superpowers founded on different ideological bases actually helped the new-founded states to live out easier the infantile period of their history.

Reliquary of "St. Matrona", silver with gilt. Bulgarian autocephalous archbishopric in Ohrid, XVIIIth C. AD

Christianity-Official Religion in Bulgaria

Chapter X

Church of the Bulgarian saint "St. Paraskeva" in Nessebur, XIVth C. AD

In 852, Khan Boris I ascended to the Bulgarian throne. After the few small conflicts with the Eastern Roman Empire and the German Kingdom (obviously the Great Powers of the age tested the young ruler), his nearly half-century-long reign brought peace with both the old and new neighbours. The brilliant Boris' diplomacy resolved all the questions at issue trough negotiations ending usually in peace and union treaties. Somewhere in the middle of his reign, Bulgaria came to the apparent paradox to be in military and political alliances with all the states in Central and Eastern Europe, which had often been implacable adversaries.

Ruins of the medieval church in Nessebur, XIVth C. AD

Actually Bulgarian ruler's love of peace was also due to the reasons that his antecedents had already reached the possible real stretch of the Bulgarian State's frontier. All the Slavs in Southeast Europe were unified within the Bulgarian frontier borders. Bulgaria was detached from the west Slavs (Poland and Czechia) and from the east Slavs (Russia) by territories occupied by non-Slavic peoples – Avarians, Pecheneges and Koumanians. Remaning loyal to the famous Bulgarian moderation, Boris I quite reasonably did not get involved in tiresome wars with those steppe peoples. Besides, the first own Slavic state formations started to appear among the western and eastern Slavs and Boris I could not expected them to naturally gravitate to Bulgaria. It had not already been the only one Slavic state.

Church "St. Virgin Mary" in Nessebur, XIVth C. AD

The "deep peace"(even the east-Roman writers called it like that) allowed Boris and his political elite to pay attention to one serious internal problem. Anticipating the events, we could say, that his determination would turn Bulgaria into civilisation centre of the Slavic peoples and states.

We were talking about the choice of one religion only, which would be

The Bulgarian tsar Ivan Alexander (1331–1371), miniature from Bulgarian manuscript, XIVth C. AD

declared official i.e. the liquidation of the typical incredible religious tolerance of the European Medieval States, which we had already mentioned. This tolerance started causing troubles. Although the Bulgarian society existed in one-nation-state, it was divided into half a dozen religious communities.

Some of the people inhabiting the Bulgarian lands were still pagans. Some of them believed in Tangra, who had been worshiped by the Bulgarians ever since they lived at the foot of the Himalayas. The pagans with Slavic origin, believed in at least couple of dozens of gods-Perun, Lada, Volos etc. The Slavic soul and imagination are really great. Other people were Buddhists or Muslims. The Christians became really a majority, especially after joining Thrace and Macedonia-completely christianised by Byzantium provinces. But they were not unified too. Besides Bulgaria came to legacy of the Christians in Thrace and Macedonia, it inherited almost all the heresies of the Byzantine orthodoxy-Pavlikians, Manikheians, Arians. "My country is full of preachers of many religions", Boris complained in his letter to pope Nicolas I.

As we know, the religious communities in the Middle Ages and even nowadays, have often been in conflict with each other. It weakens the unity of any state. Conflicts emerged even amongst the Christians of one same cult. One hagiographer from the same

Church-ossuary in Bachkovo monastery, XIth C. AD

age told a story in his work – "Biography of the martyrs of Tiveriopol", which sounded tragicomically. In the vicissitudes of the war with Byzantium, the inhabitants of a Bulgarian Christian town in Macedonia had stolen the relics from other neighbour Christian town and deposited them in their cathedral church. After the war died down, the inhabitants of the second town wanted the relics back, but those of the first one did not agree to give them back. The negotiations of both Christian communities ended in an impasse and the population of the towns, armed with whatever they found, prepared to fight – the first ones in order to defend the relics, the others to take the relics back. The governor, who had been pagan Tangra worshiper and who did not have any idea how to resolve Christian problems, was astonished. In the end, he got angry and resolved the problem in soldier manner. He made the heavy armoured soldiers intervene in both towns in order to prevent the citizens from killing each other and separated the relics into equal parts between them.

Church, built by the Bulgarian Tsar Ivan Assen II (1218–1241) in a mountain fortress above Assenovgrad

The main port and the Patriarchal church in the Bulgarian capital Tarnovo (1185–1393)

Boris I was embarrassed by something far more serious from statesman's point of view. Religious pluralism did not allow imposing common legal framework in some spheres of life on all the state's subjects. Let us examine the family law and the family property. The Animists had right to marry two wives under their religious laws, the Muslims-fourth wives. In some Christian sects both the children and women were public property. We could

Yard in the monastery near the village of Bachkovo, built in 1083

imagine what confusion had caused property and inheritance defining.

Religious tolerance had to be abolished. Boris chose Christianity out of various available possibilities to accepting official religion. It was written a lot about the motives that had determined his choice. Both the medieval Byzantine and Latin authors, greeting with enthusiasm the christianising of the third European superpower, wrote about the God's will downing on Boris in his sleep and the strong sermons of his sister – a Christian, which had convinced him that the Christian faith had been the truth one. But one really pragmatic person as Boris was, as well as his team, were influenced to great extent by rather secular statesman's motives, which played a crucial role.

Firstly, the predominant part of the population of Bulgaria had already been Christians. Making an announcement to that population that they had to start to worship Mohamed, Tangra or Perun from the next day on, was equal to revolt and sanguinary civil war.

Secondly, without any doubts, Boris I was attracted by the moral and ethic Christian values. If they were shaped in legal framework conformed to the Christian faith they would bring order in society and eliminate all the contradictions on religious and secular base. The code of laws had

The church "Christ All-Powerful" in Nessebur, XIIth C. AD

already been prepared and applied by the Christian states in Europe.

Thirdly, Boris I took into account the fact that Bulgaria was in Europe and that all the state formations on the Old Continent had already been Christian. He knew as a statesman that the strength of sword was changeable. The wars against Bulgaria, broken out for typically secular reasons, for one or another territory, in the past often turned into religious wars – "war against the unbelievers-Bulgarians". In the Middle Ages nothing evoked so strong enthusiasm in the eventual enemy but a war against "the unbelievers". By adopting Christianity, Boris I intended to eliminate this trump card of his potential adversaries in foreign policy. The public opinion believed that the war between Christian states was "disgraceful and unworthy deed". Everything possible was done in order to avoid war and, however, if a war broke out it was considerably humanised. For example, the prisoners-of-war were not killed and no one was taken slave, but after the battle they were

Lead seal of the Bulgarian Tsar Boris I–852–889

Ruins of the medieval Bulgarian fortress Nessebur, VI–XIVth C. AD

released. Because the holy Christian books said, that Christians were not allowed to hold in captivity or slavery other Christians.

So, in 863, Boris I accepted the Holy Christening, together with his whole people, and apparently for political reasons, unwilling to offend anybody, invited priests from Constantinople, the Papacy and the German Kingdom. They were supposed to convert the non-Christian part of the Bulgarian population. It was accomplished by the spring of 864. The Christianity was declared the only one allowed official religion by state decree; the Christian laws-common law for all the subjects.

But the troubles could not be avoided in deed. A rebellion burst out in some peripheral regions inhabited mostly by pagans. The lightly armed troops of the rebels managed to reach the capital Pliska and to draw up in battle order. According to both the Greek and Latin Christian authors of that time, Boris I advanced to the rebels and stayed

Shroud, XVIth C. AD-textile, gold and silver

alone in front of them unarmed, just holding the Holy Cross in his hand. He raised it highly above his head and thanks to its strength, the rebels surrendered without fighting. Within IX–XVIIth C., Christian authors from Western Europe in dozens of novels, dramas and poems described this case. Whether thanks to the miraculous might of the Holy Cross or to the help of 30 000 armoured horsemen from the capital's garrison, Boris I succeeded in breaking the resistance of the pagans and as a result Bulgaria became a Christian state.

The Bulgarian conversion to Christianity caused one external political problem. To which of the already formed administrative centres of the European Christianity (Con-stantinople and Rome) should the Bulgarian dioceses belong? Both the Roman and Greek priests practising in Bulgaria led fierce struggle against each other. Boris I himself carried on long and verbose correspondence with the pope and Constan-tinople's patriarch. Without doubt, his aim was to achieve optimal independence of the Bulgarian church as far as the church law went. After six years of negotiations, Constantinople turned out to be more generous and offered the Bul-garian church to be autocephalous (self-governing). But, here Boris I proved to be wise statesman again. Unwilling the choice to be attributed to him, he declared himself

Shroud, XVIIth C. AD-
textile, gold and silver

Icon of St. Virgin Mary,
XVIIth C. AD

incompetent on the religious deeds and expressed formally his wish the problem to be resolved by the Oecumenical council. It was held in 870. The pope's delegates turned out to be minority. Besides, when the "Bulgarian question" was raised at the end of the council, some Roman delegates had already left. The Bulgarian bishops said that they were not able to decide to whom they should be subordinated in the religious and administrative hierarchy. Then the delegate from Constantinople posed the question: "When you conquered your motherland what kind of churches and priests did you find there?. The answer was "Greek". It resolved the problem. The Bulgarian church having the rank archbishopric included seven bishoprics and was subordinated to Con-stantinople's patriarch. However, it was declared autocephalous (self-governing) i.e. the subordination was absolutely titular. It pronounced itself completely independent Patriarchy fifty-seven years later.

The Ancient Bulgarian (Slavic) Writing

Chapter XI

Evangelisation of all the Bulgarians caused another problem. But the Bulgarian statesmen had prognosticated it, they had known about it and they had been ready to meet it.

Christianity, as we know, is a religion, which could not be professed without writing and books. The Saint Gospel is written in a book. In accordance with the ecclesiastical calendar, everyday the day of one or even dozens of saint is celebrated and their saint's lives are red in church. Christianity is sermons, philosophical analysis and interpretations as well; all of them written down in a book. The information written in the Christian books is a law; any changes made in it are considered to be heresy.

During those centuries, the trilingual dogma was into force in the Christian church. In accordance with it, Christianity could be professed in the three sacred languages only-the Hebrew, the Latin and Greek. Every other Christianity professed in other language and writing was not considered as real Christianity, but heresy.

Naturally, this circumstance could not be greeted with enthusiasm over Bulgaria. The Greek was appropriate for Byzantium – the Greeks were majority of the imperial population. Even dead for a long time, the Latin

Lead seal of high medieval Bulgarian official, Xth C. AD

Lead seal of high Bulgarian state official, Xth C. AD

Lead seal of the Bulgarian Tsar Peter I (927–969)

was to some extent comprehensible at least in the Romanesque states in Europe. But the Slavic was absolutely far from all the "sacred" languages. How could the God's words and the wise sentences of the church fathers reach the ordinary people, if preached in the completely incomprehensible Greek and Latin languages? What kind of alienation between intelligence and nation would appear, if the first red and wrote in Greek and Latin but the latter knew just spoken Slavic?

Would not Byzantium-the permanent rival on the Balkans – take advantage of the fact, that both the clergy and officials had only Greek

The church "St. Virgin Mary" in Ohrid, XIXth C. AD

Entrance to the church "St. Clement" in Ohrid, XIIth C. AD

educational background, in order to create its own lobby in the Bulgarian religious and administrative life with all deriving dangers for the state?

It was clear what was necessary. Creating Slavic alphabet and achieving its canonical recognition by Rome and Constanti-nople – considered by everybody as religious leaders at that age.

The story about the creation and recognition of the Slavic alphabet and writing looked like a fairy tale. The amazing fact was that everything in it was truth, as large number of independent authentic sources confirmed.

The real creators of the Slavic alphabet were two brothers-Cyril and Methodius from the city of Thessalonica-the second biggest city in

North facade of the church "St. Sofia" in Ohrid, built by the Bulgarian Tsar Boris I in 865

144.Part of the Ancient town in Ohrid-Bulgarian capital during X–XI Th C. AD

Byzantium. They were sons of the governor of military-administrative region Tessalonica i.e. children of one of the highest aristocrats of empire. In their biographies, they mentioned themselves that they had been from "aristocratic family close to the tsar, who had emigrated to Byzantium". During this historic period, the Bulgarians were the only that had tsar. Therefore, actually, it was possible. In the middle of VIIth C. some Bulgarian rulers were dethroned after internecine struggles and forced to immigrate to Byzan-tium together with the remaining loyal aristocrats. There, they recei-ved high aristocratic ranks and administrative appointments. The excellent command of Bulgarian language of both brothers was an argument in favour of this possibility.

In compliance with their high ranks, the two brothers were sent to Constan-tinople, where they were supposed to study in Mag-

The Ancient town in Ohrid-capital of Bulgaria during X–XIth C. AD

Part of the Ancient town in Ohrid-Bulgarian capital during X–XIth C. AD

naura School. After their graduation, they both received high administrative appointments. The elder brother-Meth-odius-was appointed governor of big military-administrative region in Tessalia. Cyril, who had demonstrated early brilliant intellectual qualities, was appointed librarian-in-chief of the Patriarchy's library. This post appears too humble in these days, but in Byzantium, the future patriarch of Constantinople usually holds it.

Suddenly, to disappointment of both the patriarch and emperor, the two brothers put an end to their brilliant careers in 855, isolated themselves in a monastery announcing boldly that they had been determined to devote to the Slavic evangelisation, which could be done much easier through a writing in Slavic language. Therefore, they had been determined to create and translate the Holy Books from Greek into Slavic. They overthrew the statement that the new writing had not been canonical by using enough strong arguments: "Does not God offer sun, air and rein to all the peoples" – Cyril protested – "this is a testimony that God loves all the peo-

Lead seal of the Bulgarian Tsar Simeon the Great (893–927)

The church "St. John the Precursor" in Kurdjali, XIIth C. AD ples equally. Why do you thing, then, that God wants to be glorified in the languages of only three peoples".

The unexpected decision of the brothers Cyril and Methodius coincided strangely with the already manifested determination of Bulgarian tsar to convert himself together with his people. Therefore, it was more than sure, despite the lack of concrete pieces of information, that Boris I had shared with the two brothers his apprehensions regarding Christianity practising in Bulgaria in Greek or Latin and he had begged them to co-operate in eliminating the obstacles. Some scientists even saw romantic motives besides the so declared by Cyril and Methodius platonic affection to the Slavic people. According to them, the Bulgarian tsar's sister Ana established the connection between Cyril and Boris. There was information that she had studied with Cyril in Magnaura University. Naturally and clearly, the great love had burst out there and motivated Cyril further to take so much care of the Slaves.

By 862, both brothers invented the alphabet and translated the main liturgical books into the Slavic language. Relieved that he had a weapon, Boris I adopted the Christianity in the very next year. Naturally, he was not able to set in immediately service in Slavic language. With the speed of lightning, Rome and Constantinople would have declared him together with his whole people heretics. It was necessary to achieve canonical recognition of the Slavic writing and to teach in advance thousands of priests and teachers.

Too unexpectedly, the canonical recognition came at first from Constantinople. In same 862, the Moravian prince Rostislav,

The medieval feudal palace Matochina, XIIIth C. AD

who had adopted Christianity as well, addressed a request to the emperor to send him priests of Slavic language (his people also were not able to comprehend the Latin sermons of the sent by the pope German priests). He promised in return to include his state in the Byzantine sphere of influence. The statesmen in Constantinople decided that it would not be bad to tear one state away from the pope's sphere of influence. At the same time, they understood that if they kept on protecting the trilingual dogma it would never be achieved. Moravia was too far. There were no other means to exert influence on it. Therefore, in Constantinople, the Patriarch himself made unprecedented in the Church's history concession by blessing the new alphabet and declaring it completely canonical. On their way to Moravia, Cyril and Methodius naturally passed trough Bulgaria. Boris I entrusted to them a group of young mensons of Bulgarian dignitaries, who had to learn the new writing.

In the course of seven years, Cyril and Methodius preached in Slavic language in Moravia and desperately fought against the Latin clergy's attacks. In 869, pope Nicolas I summoned them to go to Rome where they had to give explanations. At least, because they preached in a pope's diocese. Apparently, preparations for retaliation were under way. However, before the two broth-

"St. Cyril and St. Methodius and their five disciples", fresco from the church "St. Naum" in Ohrid

Ruins of the medieval
Bulgarien fortress Pernik,
IX–XIVth C. AD

Ruins of the medieval
Bulgarien fortress Pernik,
IX–XIVth C. AD

Ruins of the medieval
Bulgarien fortress Pernik,
IX–XIVth C. AD

Ruins of the medieval church near the town of Sozopol, VI–XVIIth C.

Medieval Bulgarien church, Kosti village, Burgas region, XVIIIth C.

ers reached Rome, pope Nicolas had died. The new pope Adrian II had some troubles with his throne. Too strong circles in the Roman society were against his appointment. Searching for rivals, he wanted Byzantium to cooperate. He reali-sed that if supported the idea and the deeds of Cyril and Metho-dius, who were considered by him Byzantine agents in the pope's diocese, he would get the help that he wanted from Constan-tinople.

Therefore, Cyril and Methodius were accepted as Christian heroes in Rome instead of being offended, abused and condemned as heretics. The Slavic alphabet and writing were declared absolute-ly canonical with solemn litanies, public prayers and special service in the church "Santa Maria Magiore" and the Slavic books sanctified by the pope him-self. In 879, pope John VIII recog-nised that act too. Unfortunately, the two brothers could not see Bulgaria once again. Cyril died in Rome. Metho-dius died several years later. After Methodius died, the German clergy had forbidden the Slavic alphabet.

However, the great deed was accomplished and the torch taken by

Rila monastery

Bulgaria. The Bulgarian disciples of Cyril and Methodius-Clement, Naum, Angelarius and Gorazd-who had arrived from Moravia, and dozens of others, of whom we did not know the names, headed the leadership of Bulgarian church and culture. They introduced their mother tongue in church and founded schools in each parish region observing the resolutions of the VIIIth Oecumenical Council. Teaching in mother tongue went easy and rapidly. At

Saint Ivan Rilski – Bulgarian national saint, Xth C.

Church dedicated to the Bulgarian saint Ioakim of Ossogovo,
the town of Kriva Palanka, XIXth C.

the same age and even centuries later, the dead Latin was accepted as the only one literary language in Western Europe, which was accessible only to the clergy and some of the political persons that were devoted to it. According to the estimations of some competent scientists not more than 2–3% of the population were literate. According to the opinion of the same scientists' literacy spread over 65–70% of the Bulgarian population.

Bulgaria-Centre of the Slavic Christian Civilisation

Chapter XII

It is well known in Western Europe that the hard work of thousands Irish monks restore the positions of Christianity and writing after the barbarisation of this part of the continent in III–IVth C. These islanders, sons of ancient people have survived the massacres of the Barbaric invasions, walked across the West holding the Holy Gospel in hand, baptised the newcomers, build temples, restored old religious structures and created new ones.

In Eastern Europe, all this has been done by the Bulgarians.

Nowadays, it is difficult to find out, where the motives of the Bulgarian monks, dispersed all over the Christian world from the Odder to the Ural, have been determined solely by Christian devotion, as in Irish case. This feeling is really too strong in the newly converted. There is no information about some state operations involved in this matter. But probably some of

„Kalojan and Dessislava“ – mural painting from the church in Bojana quarter, Sofia

them have been sent by the Bulgarian State. The christianising and the Bulgarian writing naturally have created a Bulgarian sphere of influence in some Slavic state formations. But more important is that they have created "a state of spirit", in the words of the Russian academician Lihachov, which will exist even when the Bulgarian State is in political decline or even if it does not exist. The created literature and historical works are not confined within the limits of the Bulgarian literature and its needs, but they treat common human issues, which have incorporated the Slavs to the common European culture. It becomes an intermediary, which has introduced the spiritual achievement of both the Christianity and Antiquity to the south and the east Slavic literatures.

We have mentioned that monks-missionaries evangelisers of the pagan Slavs have done the distribution of Christian literature. Here is the right place to mention that immediately after Bulgarian christening, thousands of monas-

The church of "St. Stephan", Nessebur, XIIIth C.

The medieval Bulgarian fortress Mezek, Haskovo region, IX–XIVth C.

teries' lights start glittering on its territory. Thousands of monks in dozens of scriptoriums have the responsibilities to translate or multiple by copying from Greek to Bulgarian, not only the indispensable for the service holy books, but also the huge philosophical heritage left by the fathers of the Christian Church: literature works (stories, novels, hymns). The most talented (Chernorizets Hrabar, Prezviter Kozma, Constantine of Preslav, Ioan Ekzarch etc) have created original pieces with various thematic and genres. As long as the ancient works are saved in Byzantium, they have passed trough the writing desks of the Bulgarian translators and copyists as well.

Directions and "Acquired" Territories

Chapter XIII

The closest peoples on the Balkans- the Serbs and the Croatians-were the first peoples subjected to the particular Bulgarian spiritual expansion. Actually the Serbs were the first to accept Christianity (in 879) after the Bulgarians. But a little bit later, their territories became part of the Bulgarian kingdom in the vicissitudes of the grandiose war of the Bulgarian Tsar Simeon the Great (893–927) with Byzantium. Therefore,

Fortress walls of Ohrid – the medieval Bulgarian capital (997–1018)

the spreading of the ancient Bulgarian wring and literature over the Serbs happened within the frontier borders of the Bulgarian State. Serbia begun existing independently after 934, but the Slavic writing had never left it.

The destiny of the Slavic writing in the Croatian lands was more complicated. The Bulgarian monks-missionaries apparently handed it over thousands of evangelised Croatians at the end of IXth C. We wrote "apparently", because the liturgical books that they brought with them, and which were distributed to Croatia, had been written in Glagolitic alphabet i. e. the older one. Later, the Catholicism was imposed together with its service and literature both written in Latin language. However, the Glagolitic alphabet stayed forever in literature as symbol of the Croatian nationalism and national identity. Even, it reached unexpected blossoming forth in XVII–XVIIIth C. after the Trident council, when the Papacy allowed the service (even with some restrictions) to be held in mother tongues, as counteraction of the Reformation.

On their way northward and eastward to the Slavic areas, the Bulgarians had evangelised even one non-Slavic people-the Romanians. These descendants of both the Daceans and legionnaires of the Roman emperor Trajan abandoned by Marcus Aurelius in 275 in the valleys of Valachy and Moldova, were befriended carefully by the missionaries of Bulgaria. The Romanians would found their own state as late as the middle of XIVth C. The language of the church i. e. the Slavic Bulgarian language would become official state language. And It would be like that until XVIIIth C. Nowadays, the Romanian historians must know the ancient Bulgarian language, in order to be able to read, analyse, and use in their historiography both the state acts of their rulers and literature of their antecedents.The fragmentary pieces of information testified that the Bulgarian monks-missionaries penetrated among the West Slavs despite they suffered a failure there. Czechia and Poland would remain in the sphere of Catholicism and Latin language. But in 973, the pope issued a bull against the "illegal Bulgarian bishop in Prague". Many sources testified that in Krakow, a "Bulgarian bishopric", which had evangelised thousands of pagan Slavs, was active between 972–999.

However, the vast Russian areas were undoubtedly the great Bulgarian success. "The battle for Russia" would last nearly one century. Russia would officially adopt Christianity as late as 988. However, hundreds of Bulgarian missionaries would set the preconditions scattering as seeds all over Russia-from Murmansk on the Atlantic Ocean Shore to the Dnepre's mouth in the Black Sea. According to a legend, even the official adoption of Christianity was done under the imperious ordinance of the wife of the Russian Tsar Vladimir Olga, who was princess from the Bulgarian royal court. Olga acted not in a completely Christian manner. She forced the bolyars from the court to enter the Dnepre River in order to christen them, by using a whip. But what could they do? Even nowadays, the Russians admit that only strong hand could rule over our free Slavic hearts.

The distribution of Christianity and Slavic writing to Russia was of paramount importance for the expansion of Christianity and preservation of writing and literature.

The Russian expansion over one sixth of the earth in XVII–XIXth would christianise and introduce the culture of writing to all the Slavs and non-Slavs from Moscow to Vladivostok and from Arctic to China. In the West, the Russian would christianise Ukraine and Belloruss.

The "mutual salvation" of the Slavic literature in hard times was quite interesting. It was carried out between the Bulgarian and Russian territories. Between XII–XIVth C. Russia was smashed and dominated by the Tartars. The fires' flames had destroyed all the spiritual centres. Right at that moment, Bulgaria was at the top of its political might. As soon as the Battle of Kulikov ended in 1387, Bulgaria not only stopped the Tartaric rush, but also flooded recovered Russia with various pieces of literature of its scriptoriums. The Russian historians called this act "the second south Slavic influence". The first happened naturally in IX–Xth. C. between XVI–XIXth C. Bulgaria, on its turn, was conquered and dominated by the Muslim Ottoman Empire. It had already been the time of the printed book, but the intolerance of the Islamic fanaticism did not allow anyone printing house to functioning in the Bulgarian lands. Then, the wandering Russian monks flooded the Bulgarian churches and monasteries with literature. In that way, they did not let the Christian deed, done by the finger of God, to die away.

Fortress walls of Ohrid – the medieval Bulgarian capital

What Did the Bulgarians Read in the Middle Ages

Chapter XIV

We will start with the particular written language. By the time when the Bulgarians adopted Christianity in the middle of IXth C., the common Slavic language had not already existed. The national languages of the Russians, the Poles, the Czechs, the Serbs and the Croatians had already been separated and sufficiently well formed. But there was no particular lexical and grammatical difference between them. Therefore, the Bulgarian language was well enough comprehensible. However, the fact that until XIIth i. e. in the course of 300 years not one Russian or Serbian translating centre had been created, aroused bewilderment. The Russians, the Serbs and the Romanians copied the Bulgarian hand written books to the last coma in a "phototype" manner. There had happened even some curiosities. One famous literary collection of orations was copied in Russia for the Russian Tsar Svetoslav in 1092. A laudatory dedication addressed to the Bulgarian Tsar Simeon, who had ruled a century and a half before, was written on the front page. Apparently, the copied original came from the royal library. The copyists did not dare at all to lead out of the original. Probably because both the Bulgarian alphabet and literature were canonical; the beliefs that every deviation was heresy excited apprehensions. However, in XIIth C. during the period of the "second south Slavic influence", there was another return to the Bulgarian originals. This time it lasted for a shorter period.

So, what had the Slavs read in their own language. They used to read mainly translated literature. Naturally, the Bible was in the first place. As is known, the Bible includes 50 books of the Old Testament and 27 of the New Testament. Methodius in Moravia (or in Byzantium for the Moravian mission) translated them for the first time not as late as the middle of IXth. C. Presbyter Gregorius was the one to translate them for the second time in the Bulgarian capital of Preslav.

The Psalter, which was the most widespread work and at the same time compulsory for all the Christians, took a special place in this range. This collection of poetic hymns was needed during the whole day. Reading a definite number of psalms was compulsory in everyday personal and social life.

The four Holy Gospels-the base of the Christian faith-made up big part of the Slavic men of letters' literature production. Dozens of apocryphal gospels that had not been recognised by the church were in circulation at the same time.

The works of the church fathers, who had been the Christian ideologists of both the Late Antiquity and Middle Ages, made up another part of the literary wealth of the Slavic literature.

Regarding the scope of secular literature, everything possible that could be found in Byzantium was translated. As is known, Byzantium had preserved and developed in its libraries the ancient cultural tradition. Everything had been translated into Slavic. The Slavic peoples had got to know the ancient literature tradition, long before Western Europe did it. Therefore, probably the famous American medievalist Prof. Ricardo Pikio may be in his right to claim that it is more correctly to talk about "Byzantine-Slavic Civilisation" instead of "Byzantine Civilisation".

And finally – their own original works – saints' lives, divine hymns, historical works philosophical treatises and publicist's writings. Literary wealth, exceptional in genre and contents.

CONTENTS

BOJIDAR DIMITROV

BULGARIANS – THE FIRST EUROPEANS

Bulgarian
First Edition

Graphic Design Konstantin Radoslavov

St. Kliment Ohridski University Press